A POCKET HISTORY
OF IRELAND

Leinster House, now the seat of the Dáil. Originally it was
the home of the Fitzgeralds, earls of Kildare, later
(when this picture was drawn) the headquarters
of the Royal Dublin Society.

Above: Cahir Castle, County Tipperary, one of the
more intact Norman castles in the country.
Right: A beehive hut from the Early Christian
monastery on Skellig island.

A POCKET
HISTORY OF
IRELAND

Breandán Ó hEithir

THE O'BRIEN PRESS
DUBLIN

Above: The Battle of Vinegar Hill, Wexford,
which took place during the rising of 1798.
This picture was published in 1799.
Right: John Redmond led the Irish Party in
Westminster during the pre-First World War debate
on Home Rule for Ireland. Here Ulster
shows its stand on the issue.

This updated edition first published 2000 by
The O'Brien Press Ltd.,
20 Victoria Road, Rathgar, Dublin 6, Ireland.
Tel: +353 1 4923333; Fax: +353 1 4922777
E-mail: books@obrien.ie; Website: www.obrien.ie
First published 1989.
Reprinted 1990, 1991, 1992, 1993.
Updated 1996, reprinted 1997, updated 2000, reprinted 2001.

ISBN 0-86278-633-9

British Library Cataloguing-in-Publication Data
Ó hEithir, Breandán
A pocket history of Ireland. – 3rd ed.
1. Ireland – History
I. Title II. Ireland
941.5

9 10 11 12 13 14
01 02 03 04 05

The O'Brien Press receives
assistance from

Editing, layout, design: The O'Brien Press Ltd.
Cover separations: C&A Print Services Ltd.
Printing: The Guernsey Press Co. Ltd.

Contents

The First Settlers

The first settlers in Ireland, as far as is known, arrived in the mesolithic or middle stone-age period, about eight thousand years ago. They landed in the north-east – near where the town of Larne stands today – having crossed the narrow channel from Britain. They were hunters, using primitive implements.

The next colonists were farmers who cultivated the soil, raised animals and traded to a limited extent. They belonged to the neolithic, or new stone-age, period and traces of their civilisation can be seen at the folk park near Lough Gur in County Limerick, where excavations revealed homes, various implements and pottery. These people showed great reverence for the dead. In fact they constructed tombs of greater durability than the dwellings in which they lived. Many of their tombs have survived in different parts of the country. Some of these megalithic (large stone) tombs are constructed of two or three standing stones supporting one or two cap-stones. These are known as 'portal graves' or 'portal dolmens'. One of the most striking is at Poulnabrone in the Burren, County Clare. Because of the slant of the huge cap-stone it looks rather like the launching platform for a stone-age missile.

Much more elaborate is the passage grave. This consists of a burial chamber of stone covered by a huge earthen mound, with access to the chamber through a passage from the outer edge. One of the biggest of these burial mounds is on the top of Knocknarea Mountain in Sligo. It is reputed to be the burial place of Queen Maeve, the legendary leader of the province of Connacht, but the entrance has been obliterated and the excavation of the thousands of tons of rock is too daunting a task.

Newgrange

Three of these tombs, which are about five thousand years old, can be visited in the valley of the Boyne near Drogheda, just a short journey from Dublin. Newgrange, Dowth and Knowth are close together, but Newgrange is the best-known and most impressive. It is believed to be a century or two older than the first pyramid of Egypt.

The mound is 11m high and 85m in diameter and the passage is 19m long. The roof was constructed by placing layers of flat stones one on top of the other, each layer protruding inward over the one beneath it. The stones at the entrance are covered with carved abstract designs, but the mound's most interesting feature is an aperture in the roof-box over the door. This is constructed so as to admit the rays of the sun along the passage to illuminate the burial chamber on the shortest day of the year, 21 December, a much-filmed and photographed event when the sun obliges. The construction of this roof-box indicates that the builders were aware of the calendar and were probably sun-worshippers. The size of the construction shows that it was assembled by a community of some substance.

Some of the tombs at Knowth were discovered in 1967 and 1968, and further excavations are in progress there at the time of writing.

Iron Age Forts

The construction of larger fortifications belongs to the iron age – after 500 BC – and many forts of varying shapes and sizes survive. The most impressive is Dún Aengus on Inis Mór, the largest of the Aran Islands in Galway Bay. It is a huge semi-circular fort built on the edge of a sheer cliff, 300 feet (about 100m) over the sea. These forts were clearly meant to give shelter to people, and perhaps to their animals, during an attack. What is not clear is who the attackers were. Dún Aengus must have taken many years to build and, as it is some distance from fresh water, could not withstand a long siege. One recent theory maintains that these forts had little to do with defence and were centres of worship and ceremonial. It is this element of mystery, as much as its awesome aspect, that attracts visitors to Dún Aengus in great numbers.

The Grianán of Aileach, in Donegal near the border with Derry, and Staigue Fort, near Caherdaniel in Kerry, are among the most spectacular ring forts on the mainland. Dún Aengus is favoured by those whose interest in antiquities is small but who appreciate the panoramic view from the cliff-top that extends from the coast of Kerry to the farthest tip of Connemara.

The Celts

The Celts arrived from central Europe probably as early as the sixth century BC, with further groups arriving at later stages. They were reputed to be clever, good craftsmen and brave to the point of foolhardiness. Diodorus Siculus, a Roman historian, wrote of the Celts in the first century BC in a passage which is not entirely unkind to them: 'Physically the Celts are terrifying in appearance, with deep-sounding and very harsh voices. In conversation they use few words and speak in riddles, for the most part hinting at things and leaving a great deal to be understood. They frequently exaggerate with the aim of extolling themselves and diminishing the status of others. They are boasters and threateners and given to bombastic self-dramatisation and yet they are quick of mind and with good natural ability for learning …' As warriors they were no match for the Romans who, with their superior weapons and tactics, eventually drove them to the extremities of the continent.

Celtic Ireland was divided into about 150 little

kingdoms and five provinces, each with its own king. (Four of them – Ulster, Munster, Leinster, Connacht – still survive as units, mainly in sport, but the use of the name Ulster to describe Northern Ireland, which contains only six of the original nine counties of Ulster, is resented by those who take their history seriously.) There were no towns and the cow was the unit of exchange. The Celts were great believers in the extended family as a social unit. Each province was dominated by one family, but succession to the throne was determined not by primogeniture but by election. The elders of the various clans had the right to vote, and this gave rise to serious faction fighting. For this reason one writer described the Irish of that period as 'the spleen-divided Gaels'. However, the country was united by a common language and culture. Of the Celtic languages surviving today – Irish, Scots Gaelic, Welsh, Breton and, theoretically at least, Manx and Cornish – Irish is the only one with an independent state to support it.

The strongest strands in the Celtic culture, apart from the language, were religion and law. The religion was druidism, administered by a priest-hood of druids. The laws were written and inter-preted by a class of professional lawyers known as brehons. There was an elaborate code of legislation based on the community and the extended family. Fosterage of children, who were then brought up by the foster family, was common and forged links between different families. Much conflict erupted later when the Norman invaders tried to impose their totally different code.

One of the differences between the two codes concerned the status of women who, in the Celtic system, had a high standing. Women had the right to own and to inherit property and also the right to divorce. In legend, Queen Maeve of Connacht is portrayed as a warrior and a feared leader of men. In reality, Grace O'Malley, the seafaring contemporary of Queen Elizabeth I of England, made war on her enemies along the west coast on land and on sea. Known as Granuaile, she entered into marriages on her own terms and on occasions retained her partner's lands after declaring that the contract was at an end!

There was also great respect for learning, and the poet (*file*) was both admired and feared. To be lampooned by the more ferocious satirists was a fate worse than death and their patrons had to be careful not to offend them. On one occasion a poet who had been offended by King Guaire went on a hunger strike on the threshold of the palace. Even though the king came personally offering food, the poet, Seanchán, died. W. B. Yeats based his play *The King's Threshold* on this event, an early example of the hunger strike which became such a powerful political weapon in Ireland in modern times.

Christianity

In the absence of strong central authority, it is strange that, as far as can be proved, the Romans never invaded Ireland. In fact it was a raid by Irish pirates on a Roman settlement in Britain which led to the coming of St Patrick, the man who Christianised the island. Patrick, a boy of sixteen and a Roman citizen, was carried off to Ireland as a slave. He escaped eventually, and, after studying in Gaul, returned as a missionary in AD 432. He said that the children of Ireland appeared to him in his dreams appealing to him to return.

There were isolated groups of Christians in Ireland before 432, but when Patrick died, thirty-three years later, the whole island was effectively Christianised. This was accomplished so peacefully that there is no record of even a single martyr. The credit for this must be shared between Patrick, who was a natural diplomat and compromiser, and the kings who allowed him to engage in public disputation with the druids concerning the merits of their different gods.

The stories about St Patrick's mission, as they lived on in folklore, were composed many years after his death. Many of them were undoubtedly fables, but none the less powerful for that. One example is the story concerning his attempt to convert the high king of Munster to Christianity. According to this legend the saint got so carried away that he plunged his crozier into the ground, piercing the king's instep! The king was so impressed with what he assumed was part of the conversion ritual that he accepted the new faith with alacrity. However, other stories, particularly in the Irish language, portray the saint acting in a most unchristian fashion – cursing people and casting spells. These stories are more an indication of the popular imagination than they are of the reality of the saint's behaviour during his mission.

In many instances old religious practices were continued under the auspices of Christianity, which is one reason why the early Irish church developed in a different way to the system on the Continent and in Britain. The best example of how St Patrick operated is provided by Ireland's holy mountain, Croagh Patrick in County Mayo, still a place of pilgrimage for the thousands who climb to its summit on the last Sunday in July to hear mass and perform penitential exercises. Patrick travelled extensively and when he came to this mountain he found that it was an object of worship in honour of the pagan god Crom Cruach (Crom of the Reek). Having fasted on the summit for forty days – and having done battle with various evil spirits, including the devil's mother, according to folklore – he descended and told the people to continue with their pilgrimage, but that henceforth it would be in honour of the Christian god. In Irish-speaking areas the last Sunday in July is still called Domhnach Chrom Dubh – Black Crom's Sunday. This is but one example of Patrick's skill in adapting existing practice to his own mission.

Although he referred to himself in his autobiographical work, the *Confessio*, as a man of little learning, Patrick was both shrewd and humorous and the survival of so many legends and customs concerning his travels through Ireland – as well as the fact that he is one of the few religious figures still honoured by Catholics and Protestants alike – indicates that he had special gifts. St Patrick's Day, 17 March, falls in Lent, but those abstaining from drink for religious reasons are free to honour his memory – without breaking their pledge – by drinking 'An Pota Pádraic' (Patrick's Pot) that day. Needless to say the pot may be replenished frequently!

Monasteries

The typical religious centre in Early Christian Ireland was not a diocese, but a monastery. This was a group of wooden or stone huts, laid out around a stone church. Here the monks worked and prayed together under an abbot who was usually elected from the family of the founder. Some of these settlements, where the huts were of stone, can still be seen, but all the wooden structures have vanished. The most dramatic is on the little island of Skellig Michael, off the south coast of Kerry, which can be visited by boat during the summer months. It is the nesting-place of tens of thousands of sea birds, and stands 600 feet (200m) over the sea. Having climbed up a series of stone steps which were cut out of the rock by the first monks, the visitor can see the remains of the beehive huts. The little settlement also contains a number of grave-stones.

Other examples of early settlements are on Inishmurray island off the Sligo coast – unfortunately not so easy to visit – and on Inis Mhac Dara (St Mac Dara's island) off Carna in Connemara. Another most interesting early church is Gallarus oratory, west of Dingle, County Kerry. It is constructed completely of stone, without any mortar, in a development of the method used to construct Newgrange burial chamber. The roof is still completely waterproof. Gallarus is the oldest example in Europe of this type of corbelled building.

As well as bringing Ireland the Christian religion, St Patrick and those who followed him also brought the Latin language and alphabet. Before Patrick, inscriptions were in a form of writing called *ogham*, in which letters were represented by strokes cut across or on either side of a stem-line. Examples of *ogham* may be seen in the National Museum of Ireland in Dublin. True written records began in the fifth century, and Irish borrowed and transformed many Latin words, particularly those connected with ecclesiastical matters such as *sagart* (a priest

– *sacerdos*), *altóir* (an altar – *altare*) and *eaglais* (a church – *ecclesia*). The earliest literature in Irish dates from the sixth century and consists of poems composed by professional writers who were heirs to the druids. The material was recorded in manuscripts by the early Irish monks. They also wrote down literature which had been transmitted orally from the pre-Christian culture, indicating that there was no conflict between the new tradition and the old, language being a unifying factor. The monks themselves produced lyric poetry of high quality.

Mythology

The mythological saga *Táin Bó Cuailgne* (the Cattle Drive of Coolcy), which has been rendered into English by various translators, is the outstanding work from this period. As well as having literary value it also sheds important light on the composition of early Irish society. It tells of how the men of Ulster, led by Conor Mac Nessa and the Knights of the Red Branch, and aided by the heroic Cúchulainn (the Hound of Ulster), defended the north against the men of Ireland led by Queen Maeve. The general theme can be taken as an indication of tension between Ulster and the rest of Ireland, a tension more ancient than and different in origin from that which animated more recent conflicts.

The theme of tragic love was central to some of the great romantic tales written down during this

period: tales such as *Diarmaid agus Gráinne,
Deirdre agus Naoise, Liadan agus Cuirthir.* These
themes were taken by Yeats, Synge and other
writers and poets many centuries later and developed. Cúchulainn became the symbol of the heroic
Ireland of the early twentieth century and his statue
in Dublin's General Post Office, in O'Connell Street,
commemorates the insurrection of 1916. The constant
intrusion of the country's past into contemporary
events leads some critics of Irish life, domestic as
well as foreign, to assert that in Ireland there is little
talk of the future, only the present and the past,
and that the past is always central to the present.

The Vikings

The first Viking raid on Ireland took place in 795,
and its target was Lambay Island, near Dublin. In
the beginning the invaders travelled in small fleets
of long-boats, hitting coastal settlements and making off with their loot. In 837 two large fleets arrived
in the mouths of the rivers Boyne and Liffey, and
founded permanent bases. From these the Vikings
travelled inland in search of more secluded targets.
By 841 these new invaders had established fortified
settlements.

It is not as plunderers that these Danish Vikings
are best remembered in Ireland now but as traders
who gave the island towns in the modern sense,
particularly Dublin (Dubh Linn – Black Pool) which

they founded in 841. They also introduced coinage, better ship-building techniques and new styles in art, and their presence forced the Irish to unite – in 1014 a great battle was fought between the Danes and the Irish, under King Brian Ború of Munster, at Clontarf, now a suburb of Dublin. The Danes were defeated and their military power broken, but their commercial influence remained, particularly in Dublin, Wexford and Waterford, and they intermarried with the native Irish.

Treasures of the Monasteries

By this time the Irish church had established large monastic settlements and the monks had made great technical advances in the craft of illuminating manuscripts as well as in elaborate ornamentation in bronze, enamel and gold. These treasures were the loot the plunderers of the monastic settlements – both Irish and Viking – coveted. Although much was lost, enough has survived to make a visit to the National Museum of Ireland and Trinity College Library, where most of the treasures are on display, essential for anyone interested in getting a real insight into this period of Irish history.

The Book of Kells dates from the eighth century and can be seen in Trinity College Library where a page is turned every day. It is a copy of the New Testament on vellum, illustrated with intricate designs in a variety of colours. Some of the capital letters contain thousands of strokes of the quill pens with which the monks carried out their long hours of work, as well as scores of different figures of animals and men. One of the nastiest, and probably apocryphal, stories concerning Queen Victoria is that she was annoyed that she was not allowed to autograph it during a visit to Dublin.

The Tara Brooch also dates from the eighth century and is probably the most famous piece of non-ecclesiastical ornamentation from the period. It is made of silver gilt with gold filigree and amber and glass ornamentation. The Ardagh Chalice and the much more recently discovered Derrynaflan Chalice are also in the National Museum and illustrate the reluctance of the craftsmen who shaped them to leave any area undecorated. Even the stud at the bottom of the Ardagh Chalice, which would never have been seen by anybody other than the celebrant of mass, is completely covered with minute engravings.

The high cross and round tower are typical monuments of the early Christian period and with the harp and the shamrock have become symbols of Ireland. The towers are tall, slender, stone structures, built near monasteries, and while one of their functions seems to have been to act as bell-towers to summon those working at a distance from the monasteries, the doorways set high up in their sides suggest that they also served a defensive purpose at times of attack. There are fine examples of undamaged round towers at Glendalough in County Wicklow, Ardmore in County Waterford and Monasterboice in County Louth. Many of the more elaborate high crosses are covered with panels of sculpture depicting scenes from the Old and New Testaments. These panels were designed for instructional purposes at a time when illustrated books were rare. Some of the more famous are the Cross of Moone in County Kildare, the Cross of Ardboe in County Tyrone, the Cross of Monasterboice in County Louth, and the Cross of Cong in County Mayo, a shrine for a fragment of the True Cross made by order of the high king. Replicas of some of these crosses are in the National Museum.

Missionaries

The Irish monks were not solely concerned with activities at home. Many of them went abroad as missionaries, at first to Britain, where the Christian church had suffered much at the hands of the invading Anglo-Saxons. The most famous of these was St Columba or Columcille of Derry who founded the monastery at Iona in 563 after being involved in the first recorded copyright case in Irish legal history. Columba had copied a manuscript without the permission of its owner. The judgement of the court was: 'to each cow its calf; to each book its copy'. Others went farther afield: St Columbanus (not to be confused with Columba) to Burgundy and Italy; St Kilian to Saxony; St Fiachra and St Fursa to Gaul; St Livinus to the Netherlands. Irish monks settled in Iceland and although there is no historical proof for the story that it was St Brendan of Ardfert in Kerry and a group of his monks who first discovered America, the voyage of Tim Severin, in 1976-7, in a replica of the boat used by St Brendan – according to the legend – proved that such a trip was possible.

This was the golden age of Irish missionary activity but it was an activity which persisted through the centuries. Irish priests, nuns and brothers are to be found today in all the new African states, in India, Korea, the Philippines and Latin America. The Holy Ghost Fathers, who educated many modern-day African leaders, such as President Mugabe of Zimbabwe, also taught Presidents de Valera and Hillery of Ireland as well as Ireland's great lay saint of the late 1980s, pop star Sir Bob Geldof.

The Normans

Sooner or later the newly-arrived Norman-French rulers of England were bound to direct their attention to Ireland. The manner of their coming was a direct result of internal bickering and power struggles. Diarmaid Mac Murchadha, king of Leinster, had backed the losing contender for the high kingship. To compound his problems he became involved with the willing wife of a regional king and had to flee the country. He went across St George's Channel to south Wales and invited Richard Fitzgilbert de Clare, known as Strongbow, to assist him to reclaim his kingdom. The Norman adventurer came, married Mac Murchadha's daughter, Eva (Aoife), and succeeded his father-in-law as king of Leinster. (Strongbow's tomb may be seen in Christchurch Cathedral in Dublin.)

The first Normans landed in Wexford in May 1169. That was the beginning of the political struggle between England and Ireland which was to dominate Irish history until the present day. In the beginning the English crown was worried that the Norman lords who followed Strongbow would set up an independent state in Ireland. The worry was well founded, for although the invaders overcame the resistance of the native kings and chiefs, who were paying the penalty for their disunity and were not able to match the Normans' armour, their fortified castles and their ability to use horses in battle, the newcomers began to adopt Irish ways very rapidly. It was said of them that they became more Irish than the Irish themselves. They adopted the Irish language, married into Irish families, took to dressing like the natives and began to play their games. Their surnames were Gaelicised, with the Norman 'Fitz' and 'de' differentiating between the descendants of the invaders and the natives who used 'Mac' (son of) and or 'Ua' (grandson of).

The Statutes of Kilkenny

So successful was this cultural assimilation that two hundred years after the first invaders arrived the English crown was forced to take severe measures at a parliament which assembled in Kilkenny, the heartland of Norman Ireland, in 1366. Its purpose was to preserve the racial purity and cultural separateness of the colonisers, thereby enabling the English crown to retain control over them.

It is a measure of the adaptability of both the Irish and the Normans that the crown was faced with such a problem. Not only were the Normans militarily superior, but their political, social and religious systems were different from those practised by the natives. They favoured central government, intensive cultivation of walled land, inheritance through the first-born male, and large abbeys rather than small monastic settlements; and Norman French was their language. They secured their land by building castles, which functioned first as strong-points in the invasion and later as centres of control and power. The native Irish seemed to accept the new way of life as something they could, and had to, live with. Gradually, Gaelic culture prevailed and although the Normans controlled about two-thirds of the country in 1366, military might and political sophistication had not been sufficiently powerful to obliterate the native way of life.

The Duke of Clarence, son of Edward III, presided over the parliament which passed the Statutes of Kilkenny. Their purpose was to prevent further assimilation, by legal and religious penalties. The settlers were forbidden to use the Irish language. They were also forbidden to use Irish names, marry into Irish families, use the Irish mode of dress, adopt any Irish laws and play the Irish game of hurling. The measures were a failure. Gaelicisation had gone too far and by now the native population, having failed to beat the invaders on the field of battle, was in league militarily with the conquerors. By the end of the fifteenth century the English crown ruled only a small area around Dublin, known from its fortifications of earth and wood as 'The Pale' (meaning a fence or boundary). The term has lived on in contemporary politics to describe those who show little understanding of the problems of rural Ireland and whose outlook is conditioned by their metropolitan surroundings.

Norman Influence

The Norman contribution to Irish life was impressive and dramatic. They introduced the feudal system of government, with lords, vassals and serfs, as well as a graduated system of administration. It was entirely different from the paternalistic, convoluted and fragmented system of clans and tiny kingdoms which had preceded it.

Norman castles dominated large areas of countryside, particularly where the land was flat and fertile. Trim Castle in County Meath and Kilkenny Castle are fine examples of Norman architecture. Irish church architecture was also strongly influenced by the colonisers. They introduced the Romanesque style, although the Irish churches tended to be smaller than the European models. The finest example of Irish Romanesque architecture is Cormac's Chapel on the Rock of Cashel in County Tipperary. In matters of church administration they rationalised the haphazard native structures and introduced new monastic orders, such as the Cistercians.

When Henry VIII came to the English throne two new elements entered into Irish social, political and religious life. He brought the country closer to London by ruling through the crown's representative in Dublin, instead of through the now Gaelicised Norman lords who did not submit to him. This caused political tension but far greater tension and dissent were caused by the introduction of the new religion with the Reformation. Normans and Gaels found another bond in their common religion, Catholicism.

It was during the reign of Elizabeth I that the

policy of extending the rule of the Pale to all parts of the island was brought to its conclusion. Under Hugh O'Neill and Hugh O'Donnell, lords of Tyrone and Tirconnell, the old Gaelic order, having absorbed most of the first colonisers, made its last stand. It found allies in Spain, but the defeat of the Spanish Armada by the English fleet aided by the elements (despite the Reformation it was widely believed in Ireland that God, who controlled the elements, was always on England's side in times of war) was a blow to their hopes of success.

The Battle of Kinsale in 1601, in which the Irish armies and their Spanish allies were defeated, marked the beginning of a new order, though this became clearer with hindsight than it was at the time. O'Neill and O'Donnell went into exile in Europe (this exit was known as 'the Flight of the Earls') and for the first time all Ireland was governed by a strong English central administration based in Dublin. Even places as remote as the Aran Islands were garrisoned by a representative of the crown.

Ulster Plantation and Cromwell

The most far-reaching, although ultimately disastrous, policy employed to subdue Ireland at this time was the colonisation of the greater part of the province of Ulster with new settlers, mostly Scottish Presbyterians. The reformed religion did not really take root on a large scale in the rest of Ireland, mainly because of its close connection with the repressive policies of the administration. In the Irish language the new religion was described as *gallda* (foreign). The Scottish settlers and their descendants remained a people apart on the island and today are still living in a state of physical and mental siege.

This system of colonisation was known as 'planting', as the native Irish were driven off almost 500,000 acres of the best land in counties Tyrone, Donegal, Derry, Armagh and Antrim, which was then divided into large estates on which the colonisers were 'planted'. The first revolt of the Gaelic Irish against the English government and those in Ireland who now possessed their land, occurred in 1641. These forces formed the rebel assembly known as the Confederation of Kilkenny but rapidly became involved in the English civil war between king and parliament.

Cromwell and his parliamentarian army crushed the rebellion ruthlessly and large-scale confiscation of land followed. The owners were driven off about eleven million acres of land and it was given to Protestant colonists whose loyalty to the English parliament would be constant. The saying 'To hell or to Connacht' originated at this time: those who did not leave their fertile fields and travel to the poor land west of the Shannon would be put to the sword and the Puritans believed that the destination of these souls was hell. '*Mallacht Chromail*' (the curse of Cromwell) is an imprecation still in use in some parts of the country. Because he typified the militaristic mixture of religion and the lust for Irish land, spilling much Irish blood in the process, Cromwell found his permanent place in the folk-memory of hate. Stories of the massacre of men, women and children, in their hundreds, after the siege of Drogheda helped to perpetuate his reputation. The stark reality was that by the time the Cromwellian war had ended the population had been reduced to about 500,000 by famine and plague as well as by systematic butchery.

The Penal Laws

As if to ensure that the new religion would be even more strongly associated with repression in the minds of the native Irish Catholics, a new series of laws, the Penal Laws, were introduced. The Irish parliament, which was set up in Dublin, was an exclusively Protestant assembly, with the result that the Catholic majority had little or no protection under the law.

Brendan Behan's definition of an Anglo-Irishman as a Protestant with a horse contained a bitter folk-memory from this period: under one penal law an Irish Catholic was not allowed to own a horse worth more than five pounds. If he was offered that sum for any horse of his by a Protestant, he would

have to accept. The fine Gaelic lament *Caoineadh
Airt Uí Laoghaire* (the Lament for Art O'Leary) has
its origins in this law: Art O Laoghaire refused the
offer and lost his life as a result. The long lament
was composed by his wife Eibhlín Dubh Ní Chon-
aill (Black Eileen O'Connell) herself a poet and an
aristocrat.

When the Catholic King James II came to the
English throne in 1685 the situation changed some-
what and some in Ireland believed that they had
no choice but to back him in his fight to retain the
crown against the challenge of William of Orange.
All of Ireland, apart from the descendants of the
Ulster settlers, backed James, although the Gaelic
poets of the time had their doubts. They referred
to him as *Séamas a' Chaca* (James the Shit) and he
was among the first to flee after William's army
defeated his at the Battle of the Boyne in 1690. A
lady in Dublin is said to have congratulated him on
at least having won the retreat.

The victory of the Battle of the Boyne is as fresh
in the folk-memory of Ulster loyalists today as that
of Cromwell is in the province of Connacht, as a
visit to the annual 12 July commemorations will
confirm. With the passage of time they became a
display of triumphalism, but are now a show of
resolution and defiance by the beleagured. Defeat
in this war left the Catholic Irish politically helpless
and leaderless. Most of their military leaders,

among them Patrick Sarsfield, left to serve as soldiers of fortune with various European armies.

Under the Treaty of Limerick of 1691 Catholics were promised the same degree of tolerance they had had before the civil war in England. It was on this understanding that the Limerick garrison surrendered and the leaders of the Catholic army – known in Ireland as 'the Wild Geese' – went abroad. William of Orange was prepared to honour the treaty but there was no hope of getting the Protestant parliament in Dublin to ratify it, and instead it introduced even more repressive measures against Catholics.

The stone on which the Treaty of Limerick is said to have been signed is on display close to King John's Castle in that city. In Irish folk-history it is said that the treaty was broken 'before the ink in which it was writ had dried'.

The Eighteenth Century

The eighteenth century was a dismal time in Ireland. Irish Catholics were seen as a threat to political stability. It was thought that they might rally in support of a Stuart attempt to regain the English throne. The Gaelic poets prophesied the coming of the 'king over the water' who would free Ireland. They also wrote bitter laments on the passing of the Irish gentry, who had been their patrons, and complained of the ignorance of those to whom Cromwell and his successors had granted their estates. The purpose of the Penal Laws, which were directed at education and property rights as much as the practice of religion, was to keep the 'untrustworthy majority' poor and powerless. In this they succeeded for the greater part of the century.

The American war of independence was an important influence on Irish politics. The example of the American colonists encouraged the Irish Protestant ascendancy to seek a measure of colonial self-government. In 1782 the Dublin parliament, hitherto subservient to London, was granted virtual independence. Although the Irish administration was still appointed by the king, Ireland was effectively a separate kingdom, sharing a monarch with England.

One of the leading figures in this independent parliament was Henry Grattan, whose statue stands in College Green, Dublin, close to the building where the parliament sat, now the Bank of Ireland. As a result of his efforts most of the penal legislation against Catholics, some of which was also applied against the Presbyterians in the north, was repealed. But events on the continent of Europe were now having an effect in Ireland. The French Revolution, with its ideas of liberty, equality and fraternity, led to the founding of the United Irishmen in 1791. The guiding spirit was a Dublin Protestant, Theobald Wolfe Tone, who had been engaged in agitation on behalf of the disadvantaged Catholics. The United Irishmen was a secret society committed to breaking the connection with Britain through the use of force and to uniting 'Protestant, Catholic and Dissenter' under the common name of Irishman. The armed rising occurred in 1798 and was a failure, despite the military aid which Wolfe Tone obtained from the French. The only successful landing occurred in Mayo, when a French force under the command of General Humbert, landed in Killala in August 1798 – the year subsequently known in Connacht as 'the Year of the French'. After some small successes, General Humbert surrendered to the Lord Lieutenant of Ireland in September. At the beginning of October another small French expedition was captured in Lough Swilly, County Donegal. Tone was aboard the flag-ship and was taken prisoner.

He died in prison by his own hand. His name remains the most revered in the calendar of Irish republican saints. His grave in Bodenstown, near Dublin, is a place of annual pilgrimage and his statue stands on the corner of St Stephen's Green opposite the Shelbourne Hotel. He is the symbol of the patriotic Protestant Irish republican as Henry Grattan was the symbol, for a period, of the patriotic Protestant parliamentarian. The rising of 1798 was put down with much bloodshed in the two areas where it had been most successful initially:

east Ulster and Wexford. In the north it had the support of most of the Presbyterians because of official persecution which, although it was on a much lesser scale than that to which Catholics were subjected, forced them into the use of arms against the authority of the king.

Westminster saw the danger which had been averted, and decided that it was time to bring Ireland under direct rule from London once more. In 1800 the Dublin parliament voted itself out of existence – bribery and other forms of pressure and corruption were used to bring this about – and the Act of Union was passed.

The most romantic of Irish revolutionaries was Robert Emmet. He was also a Dublin Protestant and his attempt to establish a republic by force of arms in 1803 would scarcely merit mention were it not for that lethal combination which sustained Irish revolutionary movements from the days of Wolfe Tone: personal romanticism, a magnificent speech from the dock, a brutal public execution and a few ballads which are still sung today. His speech from the dock lasted almost as long as his rather pathetic rebellion, but to much greater effect. As the judge waited impatiently to pass sentence of death, Emmet spoke the words that gained him his place in the calendar of republican martyrs: 'Let no man write my epitaph: for as no man who knows my motives dare now vindicate them, let not either prejudice or ignorance asperse them. Let them and me rest in obscurity and peace, and my tomb remain uninscribed, until other times and other men can do justice to my character. When my country takes her place among the nations of the earth, then, and not till then, let my epitaph be written.'

For the remainder of the century, Irish nationalist politicians and agitators campaigned for three main objectives: Catholic emancipation, which meant equal rights with Protestants in all respects; Home Rule, meaning the re-establishment of a parliament for the whole of Ireland with a relationship – not clearly defined – with the English crown; and the ownership of the land for the people who worked it, which would be the reversal of the feudalism introduced by the Normans.

Daniel O'Connell

From 1801 onwards Irish members of parliament sat in Westminster where they formed a small, ineffectual group without any power. Despite persistent agitation, Westminster was unwilling to grant major concessions to Catholics. In Ireland the memory of the risings of 1798 and 1803 kept small hopes of eventual freedom alive and Emmet's speech from the dock was recited at many a fireside – but not, one imagines, at the O'Connell fireside in Derrynane, in south Kerry, close to Skellig

Michael. Despite being barred from most professions and from parliament, a Catholic trading class was growing in the country and Daniel O'Connell was to win it status and legality.

He was educated in France through the good offices of an uncle who was a successful smuggler. Soon he became a noted advocate. His experiences of the excesses of the French Revolution are said to have turned him against physical force as a means of achieving political aims. He also killed a man in a duel and this affected him profoundly. He was a born reformer who understood the politics of the mass movement and started one called the Catholic Association. In 1829 he was elected to a parliament from which his religion excluded him. As a Catholic he could not take the mandatory oath of supremacy acknowledging the crown as head of the established church. The English government decided that it would be prudent to yield to increasing pressure on this issue, from English Catholics as well as from Irish, and it abolished virtually all disabilities against them. Henceforth, the Catholic clergy became a potent force in Irish politics and O'Connell became known as the 'Liberator'.

Having achieved Catholic emancipation, O'Connell then set out to secure his place in Irish history by restoring a parliament to Dublin. This he hoped to achieve by means of another mass movement, called the Repeal Association – meaning the repeal of the Act of Union. Mass meetings, some attracting hundreds of thousands of people, led to the English government's decision to have a confrontation. They rightly suspected that O'Connell was no revolutionary and would back away from a confrontation which might lead to bloodshed and loss of life. They banned a great rally which was planned for the site of the Battle of Clontarf, where Brian Ború had defeated the Danes. O'Connell behaved as the English government had anticipated: he called off the rally in the interests of peace and public order. This ended his authority in Irish politics. The mass of his followers, their hopes raised by the previous success of O'Connell's tactics and his promises of greater things to come, began to desert him.

Young Ireland

Already in 1840, three years before the planned Clontarf rally, other voices were being raised in opposition to O'Connell's policies. A small group of idealists formed the Young Ireland movement. Prominent among them was a Protestant from Cork called Thomas Davis, a poet and journalist, who expressed a concept of nationality similar to that outlined by Tone but with greater emphasis on Irish culture. Davis died young (his statue dominates Dame Street in Dublin) and the token insurrection staged by the movement in 1848 was almost farcical.

Still, the movement's ideals lived on, mainly because of the influence of their newspaper *The Nation*. Among other things it attacked O'Connell for having turned his back on the Irish language, which was his mother tongue. O'Connell was a pragmatist in most matters and saw the country's political future being advanced by the espousal of English as the national language. He did, however, use Irish to good advantage in the courts, and folklore is full of stories concerning his successes as a defence lawyer and of how he used his mother tongue to confound his opponents.

The Famine

A terrible national calamity which decimated the population and all but killed the Irish language (the everyday speech in areas ravaged by famine) was now occupying everyone's attention. The great potato famines of 1845-51 reduced the population from 8 million to 6.6 million through starvation, disease and emigration to Britain and America. The Napoleonic war in Europe had led to the growth in tillage farming to supply the armies. When it ended in 1815 it had a marked effect on the Irish economy. The potato had become the staple food for most of the rural population, but with the war's end came a change from tillage to pasture. This caused much unemployment and the unemployed depended entirely on small patches of sub-divided land to grow enough potatoes to sustain them. The population had increased to 8 million, two-thirds of them depending on agriculture, much of which was at minimal level. When the potato crop was destroyed by blight the result was devastating: the people's only source of food was gone.

Although the government in London was aware of the threatening problem, Ireland was not a major preoccupation and the famine had assumed the proportions of a crisis before relief schemes were implemented on a large scale. Even when they were it seemed that the crisis was of secondary importance when it came to preserving the economic policies of the day. These policies were based on the principle of non-interference with market forces in economic matters. Although the potato crop failed, the country was still producing and exporting more than enough grain crops to feed the population. But that was a 'money crop' and not a 'food crop' and could not be interfered with. The relief schemes were frequently hastily thought up, and parts of Ireland still contain roads that lead to nowhere in particular – built during the famine. These are known as *bóithre na mine* (meal roads) in Irish because a day's work was paid for with imported Indian meal. Other relief schemes were organised by proselytising Protestants who handed out food accompanied by religious tracts. Some Catholics did convert to the Protestant faith and were promptly christened 'soupers' (from the soup kitchens run by the proselytisers) as a mark of contempt by their stauncher fellow Catholic neighbours.

The famine, one of the greatest disasters to happen in a European country in peace time, was a tragic condemnation of the Union, for the dilatory manner in which the crisis was dealt with in London was a result of sheer ignorance. The *Times* of London wrote the obituary of the Irish nation by declaring that soon an Irishman in his native land would be as rare as an American Indian in his.

The Fenians

It was not just the famine itself, horrible as it was, but the national decline it precipitated that makes it the bitterest folk-memory of all. For one thing, it brought about, in a matter of years, changes that would otherwise have happened over as many decades. By 1911 the population had fallen to 4.4 million and emigration had created another Ireland in Britain and across the Atlantic in America. The Irish in America were quick to organise and become a force in American politics. Many of them also remained involved in Irish affairs, at one remove, determined to aid any attempt to overthrow British rule in the country they and their ancestors had to leave. The Irish in America were instrumental in founding the most persistent revolutionary organisation of all, the Fenian Brotherhood, which became the Irish Republican Brotherhood (IRB), from which grew the Irish Republican Army (IRA). The Fenian Brotherhood, which was named after a band of mythical heroic warriors, was founded in a Dublin timber-yard on St Patrick's Day 1858, with 400 American dollars to sustain it. Like the United Irishmen, its members were bound by oath to secrecy and loyalty to the Irish Republic.

From the beginning it was condemned by the Catholic Church. In 1865, the Archbishop of Dublin, Paul Cullen, wrote to Rome: 'If the Fenians will acquire influence among us, religion will suffer and the Mazzinian doctrines will achieve more than that which was achieved by the Anglican heresy.' The doctrines referred to were basically republican, nationalist and anti-clerical. The Bishop of Kerry, Dr Moriarty, said that 'Hell was not hot enough or Eternity long enough' to punish the Fenians. The opposition of the Church was part religious, part political. It was sinful to take an oath to overthrow the established order by force and become a member of a secret society. But having achieved political power through the efforts of Daniel O'Connell, and therefore a double hold on their flock, the Irish Church feared the secularist threat of the Fenians. However, many of the younger clergy supported the Fenians secretly and most of the Fenians were staunch Catholics who happened to have strong views on the role of the Church in Irish politics. The hostility of the Church did little to harm the Fenians and they continued to grow in strength. They even infiltrated the British army and navy in great numbers. But their rising in 1867 was a military failure and the organisation was hard pressed to survive to help prepare the ground for more successful revolutionary organisations.

Its great strength, as a secret society, which was also its fundamental political weakness, was that its aim was not encumbered by social policies. It merely wanted the British out of Ireland and a republican government established. After their rising failed, the Fenians sought other movements which would provide cover for further activities and bring them into contact with young men who would be recruited for that purpose. They became involved in the Land League, which was founded in October 1879, and gave it a degree of militancy and physical violence which it might otherwise have lacked.

Parnell and the Land League

Although the Land League was founded by Michael Davitt, an ex-Fenian with a socialist outlook, the real political leadership was provided by Charles Stewart Parnell, a Protestant landlord on a small scale and a shrewd tactician inside and outside parliament. The war for the recovery of the land of Ireland for the people of Ireland, against the landlords and the British government, was fought with a minimum of violence; although many violent incidents did occur.

One of the most effective tactics used during the struggle – boycotting – gave a new word to the English language which was borrowed by many others. It was first applied to Captain Boycott, a landlord's representative in Ballinrobe, County Mayo, and was recommended by Parnell for use in all disputes. In short, boycotting meant that nobody would have social or commercial contact with the person in dispute, or with anyone who continued to serve him in any way. For instance, in County Clare a ballad is still sung about the 'Three Brave Blacksmiths' who went to jail rather than shoe horses belonging to a man who bought a farm which the Land League wished to see shared among the smaller, poorer tenants in the locality. Such a person was known as a 'grabber' and such farms are still referred to as 'grabbed land'.

A series of Land Acts bought out the landlords and the land was returned to the tenants, who became land-owners. This was not the result desired by Davitt, who favoured the nationalisation of land. The short-term result of the war for the land was that it created a body of men and women who were skilled in the politics of agitation, as well as in the conduct of local and parliamentary politics. In the long term it created in Ireland what one commentator described as 'twenty-acre capitalists', independent and conservative in outlook, particularly after political independence had been achieved for twenty-six of the thirty-two counties of Ireland.

Having won the war for the land, Parnell looked to be on the brink of achieving his real goal, Home Rule – the new term for Repeal (of the Act of Union). His brilliant use of the balance of power that the Irish Party held between the Tory and Liberal parties in Westminster, as well as his veiled threats that if the British government did not deal with him it would have to deal with 'Captain Moonlight' (his term for the more extreme Fenians whom he was barely able to contain), allied to the grip he had on the people, meant that Parnell almost succeeded. He was known as 'the uncrowned king of Ireland'. When the British government attempted to use the Vatican to drive a wedge between the Catholic Church and Parnell, the slogan 'Our religion from Rome: our politics from home' was coined. It summed up the Fenian attitude, but it was one shared by the vast majority of the people at the time. When the time came for the annual collection for the papal funds – known as 'Peter's Pence' – another slogan was coined: 'We'll turn Peter's Pence into Parnell's pounds'.

It was from this position as the most powerful political leader of the century that Parnell fell. He lost both grace and power because of public disapproval of his love for a married woman, Kitty O'Shea, whose husband named Parnell in a divorce petition. The British establishment, led by William Gladstone, the Liberal prime minister who seemed to get on so well with Parnell, turned against him when he refused to resign the leadership of the Irish Party. A majority of the party voted in favour of his resignation, but he refused to stand down. Then the Catholic Church in Ireland attacked him publicly as an adulterer unfit for public life. Parnell fought back as best he could and some members of the party stood by him, including John Redmond who was later to lead a reunited party in Westminster.

Parnell died suddenly in 1891, and his death served only to increase the bitterness. It seemed to his supporters that he had been hounded to death by the forces of reaction, in response to the attitude of the British establishment that feared and hated him. The Fenians organised his huge funeral in Glasnevin cemetery, Dublin, where he is buried in the shadow of the round tower which marks O'Connell's grave, under a large block of Wicklow granite. Their statues stand at opposite ends of O'Connell Street in Dublin, and the inscription on the Parnell monument counsels that 'No man can sct bounds to the march of a nation.'

The fall of Parnell and the bitterness that followed was a turning point in Irish history. With the benefit of hindsight it can be said that his Home Rule bill might have started a process of independence from Britain while retaining the unity of the people of Ireland as a whole. It would have been a difficult process, for despite his Protestant faith the Unionists of north-eastern Ireland were deeply distrustful of his nationalism. However, no better opportunity was to occur in parliamentary politics in the years that followed.

The period of political stagnation that followed his death and the deterioration of political standards is well portrayed in literature by James Joyce, particularly in one powerful scene in *A Portrait of the Artist as a Young Man* and the short story 'Ivy Day in the Committee Room'. The scene in *A Portrait* takes place during the Christmas Day dinner in the Joyce household and builds up to a bitter argument between a woman who lives with the family and Mr Casey, a friend of James Joyce's father. It ends with the woman leaving the table shouting: 'Devil out of hell! We won! We crushed him to death! Fiend!', while Mr Casey breaks down in tears, sobbing: 'Parnell! My dead king!'

Yet, out of this stagnation came the forces which were to dominate the next phase of the struggle for political independence for the whole island, as well as the forces in the loyalist community which were to frustrate that nationalist aim.

The Gaelic Revival

Some of the organisations which emerged about the turn of the century were, consciously or unconsciously, preparing for what is now known as the war of independence. The Gaelic Athletic Association (GAA), of which Parnell was a patron, was founded in 1884 to promote the native games of hurling and Gaelic football and to bring athletics to the masses. It was an instant success and at an early stage in its history some Fenians attempted to take it over. The attempt failed and the organisation remained broadly nationalistic in outlook, although it did prove to be a fertile recruiting ground for the IRB. The GAA grew to be one of the most successful amateur sports organisations in the world.

The Gaelic League was founded in 1893 by the son of a Protestant clergyman from Roscommon, Dr Douglas Hyde, with the purpose of reviving interest in the native language. Irish had been in steady decline since the famine and the heavy emigration that followed it, as the poor areas along the west and south coasts, where Irish was the dominant language, were among those most affected by the national disaster. When the National School system was established in the 1830s, Irish was

49

a forbidden subject. To aid its effort to obliterate the Irish language, the system enlisted the help of parents by getting them, every time their children spoke Irish, to put a notch in sticks (known as tally sticks) issued to the pupils. The children were suitably punished at school according to the number of notches on the stick. A similar system was used in Wales against the use of Welsh.

The Gaelic League's first great success was to have Irish made an essential subject in the entrance examination to the National University of Ireland. However, Dr Hyde's effort to keep the Gaelic League non-political, open to both those who favoured political independence and those who were more concerned with promoting Irish as a unifying factor in the island, failed when the IRB succeeded in gaining control of the organisation and committing it to political independence. This decision, like the GAA's 'ban' on games they deemed to be 'foreign' (e.g. rugby and soccer), had the effect of excluding many Protestants (who would have been Unionists but cultural nationalists) from both organisations.

The GAA 'ban' was introduced with the purpose of excluding those who played the games associated with the British Army and the police force. It was continued long after the independent Irish state was founded and was not abolished until 1971. Before that, players could not play hurling or

Gaelic football as well as soccer or rugby without risking a term of suspension from the GAA. A similar rule excluded members of the RUC (Royal Ulster Constabulary) from the GAA.

The Irish National Theatre was established in the Abbey in Dublin under the patronage of an Englishwoman, Miss Annie Horniman. The major influences on its growth and development were Lady Gregory and W. B. Yeats, both of whom wrote plays for it. Its success was aided by many public controversies, the first major one concerning J. M. Synge's play *The Playboy of the Western World* which caused a riot. The riot was a result of the genuine anger aroused in some nationalists by the manner in which Christy Mahon, the Playboy, became a popular hero for having murdered his father (although he had not killed him at all and the father actually appeared in the play). The use of the word 'shift' was also deplored on the grounds that the decent Irish peasants portrayed in the play would not speak of such an intimate garment in mixed company.

As part of the burgeoning sense of Irishness, a separate trade union organisation was formed. There was also a strong Irish literary revival, powered by a revival of interest in the old Irish sagas and folk-tales, as well as a general feeling of Irishness not always nationalistic or political. In general the emphasis was on things that marked Ireland as different from

England. But among a majority of Irish people there was also a feeling that Ireland should be run by the people of Ireland; a feeling that grew out of the successful outcome of the land war.

But these currents were not yet a force in parliamentary politics. The reunited Irish Party at Westminster had the backing of the vast majority of voters. Under the leadership of John Redmond the party succeeded in getting a Home Rule bill through Westminster. The promise was that it would be implemented as soon as the World War, which began in 1914, was over. Some people in Ireland were doubtful; many others believed John Redmond's pledge and joined the British Army to 'fight for the freedom of small nations'. A minority prepared to fight for causes closer to home.

Volunteer Forces North and South

The Ulster Volunteer Force (UVF) was founded in the north-eastern counties of the province to fight against Home Rule. Mainly through the organisational skills of Edward Carson, a Dublin-born lawyer, the illegal army imported arms and began to drill openly. The slogans were 'Ulster will fight and Ulster will be right' and the more succinct 'Not an inch'.

In the rest of Ireland, and in the nationalist area of the north, an Irish Volunteer Force was established as a reaction to the UVF. Its role was no clear at the outset, but it also imported arms illegally and began to drill. It was noticeable that the British Army's attitude towards these events varied greatly. While little or nothing was done to curb the gun-running activities of the UVF, an attempt was made to seize the Irish Volunteer guns landed near Dublin in 1914. When it failed, the military, faced by a jeering and stone-throwing crowd, opened fire and killed three civilians.

Unlike the UVF with its clear aim, the Irish Volunteers were led by an uneasy coalition of Redmondite moderates and nationalists, such as Eoin Mac Neill and Bulmer Hobson, who favoured eventual independence. This faction also contained an element that favoured armed insurrection at the first opportunity. A split was inevitable and when it came, as a protest against Redmond's speeches urging men to join the British Army, a majority followed Redmond: only 11,000 out of a total of 180,000 members followed MacNeill. The minority retained the name Irish Volunteers and the others became known as National Volunteers.

Other forces had already asserted themselves. Sinn Féin (We Ourselves) was a political movement preaching self-reliance – but certainly not revolution – founded by Arthur Griffith in 1908. He advocated the withdrawal of Irish MPs from Westminster and the establishment of an independent Irish parliament, but with an external relationship with Britain through the crown.

Jim Larkin, the Labour leader, took on one of the city's biggest employers when he called the transport workers out on strike. The employer, William Martin Murphy, also owned one of Dublin's daily newspapers. The year 1914 is still remembered in the city as the year of that bitter and violent industrial dispute. To show that the movement for Irish independence was not a seamless garment, Arthur Griffith opposed the workers' demands for better wages and conditions, as well as their militant tactics which led to the establishment of the Irish Citizen Army, also dedicated to separatism. The manner in which the police were used to help break the strike turned the working classes of Dublin against them, as playwright Seán O'Casey noted in his autobiography. Soon the Citizen Army was drilling openly with the Irish Volunteers, with the British security forces keeping their distance and observing.

The 1916 Rising

It was a small group inside the Irish Volunteers supported by James Connolly, the socialist leader of the Citizen Army, that decided on asserting Ireland's independence in arms before the World War ended. They were not all members of the IRB although that organisation provided the major impetus. The Easter Rising of 1916 had an influence on modern Irish history that could not possibly have been assured at the time, although it was the outcome devoutly desired by its leaders. They were almost totally devoid of military experience and were mainly teachers and writers, like Patrick Pearse (the most influential man among them, although little known outside of Dublin), Thomas MacDonagh and Joseph Mary Plunkett, trade unionists like James Connolly, and an old Fenian, Tom Clarke, who had a small tobacconist's shop in Dublin and was symbolic of the continuity of the separatist tradition. They were all idealists who subscribed to the ideals of Tone and an independent Irish republic.

Their aims were set out, in general terms, in a proclamation which promised that in the republic all the children of the nation would be cherished equally'. The proclamation is inscribed on a statue of Cúchulainn, the mythical Ulster hero, in the General Post Office in O'Connell Street, Dublin, which was the headquarters of the insurgents.

Whatever slight chance of military success the rising had was ended before a shot was fired. A shipment of German arms, organised by Sir Roger Casement, was intercepted off the coast of Kerry by British naval forces, some days before the rising, and the ship was scuttled. This meant that the Volunteers who were to effect the insurrection outside the capital were left without arms.

Then the nominal commander-in-chief of the Irish Volunteers, MacNeill, who had been kept in the dark by the conspirators, found out accidentally about the rising of which he did not approve. National manoeuvres were to be held during the Easter weekend and this was to be the signal for the rising to commence on Easter Monday. MacNeill issued an order countermanding the manoeuvres and it was published on the front page of the country's principal Sunday newspaper.

There was confusion, but Pearse, Connolly, Clarke and the other leaders decided to stage a rising on Easter Monday. Pearse in particular believed that what he saw as 'the failure of the last generation' had to be redeemed by a 'blood-sacrifice'. He used the same rhetoric in the cause of Irish nationalism as was being used by the leaders of the imperialist forces engaged in the World War. On Monday morning the General Post Office and other centres in Dublin were occupied and the rising began. As the British government's representatives in Ireland were taken by surprise, the insurrection was not put down until Friday when Pearse surrendered ceremonially under the battered portico of the post office. Outside Dublin there was little military activity. The whole affair was a military failure that had little public support or sympathy. The rising was seen by many as a blow against the more modest aim of Home Rule and a stab in the back to those who had gone to fight in the war. After the surrender, prisoners were spat on and abused on their way to prison camps in Britain.

It was the reaction of the British authorities to the rising that guaranteed its longterm success and made the virtually unknown men who led it national heroes. The jailing of hundreds of young Volunteers, many of whom had taken no part at all in the rising, caused anger and resentment, and the execution of sixteen of the leaders – including the wounded James Connolly, who had to be placed in a chair to face the firing-squad – changed the mood of the country completely. When the World War ended and Home Rule was not granted it seemed to many that those who had staged a fight for independence in Ireland had been vindicated. George Bernard Shaw was among those who warned the British government against, in Shaw's own words, 'canonizing their prisoners'. Too late the British authorities realised that Ireland was coming under a new influence, what one historian has described with hindsight as 'the tyranny of the dead'. Those who had led the rising of 1916 knew that their gesture would probably fail, but hoped that their own sacrifice would inspire a renewal of national resistance to British rule. They also hoped that an independent Irish government would later recognise the rebellion as being justified – this approach to history persists among armed revolutionaries in many countries around the globe.

In the aftermath of the rising, a wave of nationalistic fervour swept the country and, in a general election held in 1918, Sinn Féin completely eclipsed the Irish Party. Then its elected members, instead of going to Westminster, set up an illegal assembly in Dublin called Dáil Eireann (assembly or parliament of Ireland). Some of those elected were still in jail after the rising and on their release they returned home to be met by cheering crowds. Among those elected was a heroine of the rising, the Countess Markievicz, who, although she never took her seat, earned the distinction of being the first woman ever elected to Westminster. She was also made Minister for Labour in the first illegal government elected by the first Dáil.

Women were very active in the struggle for independence. Cumann na mBan (Society of Women) was a counterpart of the Volunteers and many members were sent to jail. This continued a tradition begun during the land war, when a sister of Charles Stewart Parnell, Fanny, founded the Ladies' Land League, an organisation condemned by the Catholic bishops for being unladylike and extreme.

On the day the first Dáil met in January 1919 – without the 26 Unionist members, the 6 Irish Party members and only 25 of the 69 Sinn Féin members (the missing ones being either in jail or ill) – a group of men ambushed a consignment of explosives and shot dead two policemen who were guarding it at Soloheadbeg, County Tipperary. Their action was not sanctioned by the Dáil, nor did the majority of members approve of it at the time, but it was the beginning of the war of independence. It was also an example of military action against the forces of occupation, illegal according to the law as it stood, but which would be given retrospective justification by a native government.

The War of Independence

The war of independence was fought on two fronts, political and military, but in fact the military struggle was very much a political war which neither side could win in the field. The more extreme and repressive the measures taken by the forces of occupation to crush resistance, the more these measures were used against the British government in the propaganda war internationally but particularly in the United States. Dáil Eireann's illegal government was presided over by Eamon de Valera, a young teacher who had been born in New York to an Irish mother and a Spanish father. He had commanded a garrison in 1916 and been sentenced to death. His reprieve was probably due to a reluctance on the part of the British to execute an American citizen. Between 1919 and 1921 he spent a lot of time in the USA getting financial and political support for the movement for independence.

The armed struggle became a conflict between terror and counter-terror, with publicity playing a great part as world opinion was influenced by the tactics used by the British government to bring Ireland under military control. The indiscriminate shooting of civilians and the burning of whole streets as reprisals for the shooting of British soldiers had an adverse effect on public opinion in Britain as well. The introduction of a para-military force to strike terror into the IRA (as the illegal army was now known) and those who supported them was a last desperate effort by the British military establishment to gain a military victory. This force – known as the Black and Tans because of the mixture of police and military uniforms its members wore – did a lot to descredit British rule in Ireland. Their lawless tactics were resented by members of the Royal Irish Constabulary, many of whom resigned from the police force in protest, as well as by many officers in the regular army.

Michael Collins, another survivor of 1916, organised his own IRA undercover agents to fight British intelligence and used them as ruthlessly as his opponents used their more sophisticated resources. It was a far cry from the lofty idealism of 1916 as spies were shot down in the street and even a middle-aged woman, who was found guilty of sending information about IRA activity to the British authorities, was sentenced to death by an IRA courtmartial and shot in a bog in the middle of the night. Fighting on any continuous scale was confined to areas where the terrain suited the movements of small groups of IRA men, known as 'flying columns', who ambushed the British forces and the RIC (Royal Irish Constabulary) when they ventured out from their barracks. The IRA's most spectacular successes in the field were gained in West Cork under the leadership of Tom Barry, who had got his military training in the British Army.

World opinion was probably more affected by the death of one man than it was by the losses suffered by the British military and para-military forces. Terence MacSwiney was lord mayor of Cork and after his arrest and conviction in dubious circumstances he went on hunger strike, saying that it was not those who inflicted most suffering but those who could endure most who would triumph eventually. His hunger-strike lasted seventy-three days, but long before his death and huge funeral he had become another hero of the new Ireland. His hunger strike had also become a big international news story and had great influence on emerging leaders of Indian nationalism, particularly Mahatma Gandhi.

Negotiations

Gradually, as local government and even the work of the courts were taken over by the Dáil and as world opinion hardened against Britain, talks between the two sides began, and in 1921 a truce was declared to enable a delegation from Dáil Eireann to discuss a settlement with a British delegation led by the prime minister, David Lloyd George, and having Winston Churchill as one of its members. The Irish delegation was led by Arthur Griffith and Michael Collins, and the absence of Dáil Eireann's most able negotiator, Eamon de Valera, who chose to stay in Dublin, is still debated in Ireland. His absence was likened by one contemporary politician to a team taking the field without its best player. De Valera's attitude was that his place was in Dublin with the rest of his cabinet, as any agreement would have to be put to Dáil Eireann before it could be signed. That did not happen, as the Irish delegation felt that the final decision was in their hands. They were encouraged in their belief by Lloyd George, who used a combination of persuasion and threat to force concessions from a disunited delegation. Eventually, he issued his threat: either they signed without reference to Dublin or else he would order the resumption of what would be an 'immediate and terrible war'. The result was a disaster from the Irish viewpoint and that was apparent immediately. But in the long term it was a disaster from the British viewpoint also, although it would take various British governments many years to acknowledge its central failing.

The representatives of Dáil Eireann and the British government were only two of the parties involved in the resolution of the Irish problem. The northern loyalists had their own strong views and had powerful allies in Britain. In typical fashion, Lloyd George attempted to call their bluff by trying to force them into an agreement with the south, but he failed. After that the two main issues to be decided, from the British point of view, were that the northern loyalists were not to be coerced into a united Ireland and that whatever the nature and composition of any new southern state would be, it would have to remain inside the British Empire. Privately, the Irish delegation was assured that a small northern state would not be viable in the long term and would not survive.

The Treaty

The Anglo-Irish Treaty of 1922 was signed under threat. It was a threat that had to be taken seriously because the IRA was scarcely equipped to meet it and the civilian population was becoming war-weary. A republic consisting of the whole of Ireland, which many members of the IRA thought they were fighting for, was abandoned and six of the nine counties of Ulster were granted the status of a separate state, under the British crown and with its own parliament. The other twenty-six counties were to become a 'Free State', with the same rights under the crown as Canada or Australia. Britain was also to retain three naval bases in the new state.

When the treaty was debated by the Dáil it was the abandonment of the ideal of a republic, as well as the oath of allegiance to the crown which members of the new parliament would have to take, rather than the partitioning of the island, that dominated the bitter debate. One reason for this was that the new northern state was seen as having no economic future and that reunification would come about automatically in time: a view close to that used by the British negotiators to reassure their Irish counterparts. After a prolonged debate, a vote was taken and the treaty was accepted by a majority of seven. New elections were then held to what republicans saw as an illegal assembly, as it had been forced on them by Britain.

The country was divided into 'treatyites' and republicans, with the Labour Party and some independents trying to seek middle ground but supporting the treaty. After the election, the Dáil contained 93 pro-treaty members and 33 anti-treaty Sinn Féin members, who refused to take the oath to the British crown and stayed away. It is interesting to contrast the narrow majority in favour of the treaty in the Dáil with its composition after the election. But the election did nothing to end the argument, for even before it was held in June 1922, the new state was already on the brink of civil war.

The Civil War

The Irish civil war began on 28 June 1922 when the newly-created Free State army attacked the republican forces' headquarters in the Four Courts in Dublin with artillery borrowed from the departing British Army. Although various attempts were made to avert it, the gap between the committed republicans who took over the Four Courts and those who supported the treaty was too wide to bridge. Only Michael Collins, who had told a friend after he returned from London that what he had signed was his own death-warrant, retained some credibility with his opponents.

His efforts at peace-making aroused alarm in London and it was made clear to him by Churchill, who had been given the task of making the treaty stick, that no compromise with the republicans was possible. Churchill went so far as to offer him aircraft, which would be painted in the colours of the Free State forces, to bomb the Four Courts garrison into submission.

The republican side had no military plan and seemed prepared more for martyrdom than for victory, sustained by the oath they had taken when they joined the IRA. Although greater in numbers than the Free State army, their equipment was inferior. But the Free State army knew the terrain as well as their opponents did and soon there were no safe havens left for the disorganised and dispirited republicans.

It was a war distinguished by acts of calculated cruelty on both sides. Seventy-seven republicans were executed by the new government, many of them as reprisals and without trial. There were so many prisoners taken at one stage that the Free State government thought of asking the British for facilities on St Helena to accommodate them. Less than a year after it started, the civil war was over, without any formal surrender by the republicans. Frank Aiken, their chief-of-staff at the time, issued an order to dump arms – and it was clear that they were to be used at another time. Eamon de Valera, who was more of a republican figurehead than an active participant in the fighting, was arrested and imprisoned. Many others surrendered in despair.

After their release from jail, many republicans found it difficult to find work in an economically depressed and hostile country. There was heavy emigration to the United States and many of these embittered men and women continued to support the IRA in its efforts to establish a republic for all Ireland by force. Many of them and their descendants would today be supporters of the Provisional IRA's campaign in Northern Ireland. They would be supporters of NORAID (Northern Irish Aid), a fund-raising organisation which raises money to aid prisoners' dependants in Northern Ireland, according to its leaders, but whose resources, according to the Dublin and London governments, support the IRA.

With the exception of the Labour Party, which was founded by James Connolly in 1912, all the political parties represented in Dáil Eireann today grew out of the struggle for independence and its aftermath. When Sinn Féin split over the treaty, those who supported the treaty founded the Cumann na nGaedhael (Club of the Irish) party which later became the Fine Gael (Family of the Irish) party. This party formed the government of the Irish Free State until 1932, with the Labour Party and some independent members forming the opposition.

Sinn Féin followed a policy of abstention, refusing to enter the Dáil, which they regarded as an unacceptable assembly representing only part of Ireland, and they would not take the required oath of allegiance to the crown. After his release from jail, it became increasingly clear that de Valera, the party leader, was not convinced of the wisdom of this policy. In 1926 he and his followers split with Sinn Féin on the issue of abstention and formed a new party, Fianna Fáil (Soldiers of Ireland).

At first, Fianna Fáil members refused to take the

detested oath and remained outside of Dáil Eireann, until new legislation, introduced after the assassination of the Minister for Justice, Kevin O'Higgins, forced then to take their seats or lose them. De Valera and his party signed their names in the book that was presented to them, while asserting that they were taking no oath but engaging in what de Valera called 'an empty formula'. This tactic caused one historian to call de Valera 'the political Houdini of his day'. Many others saw this and subsequent actions of his as confirming Collins' description of the treaty as 'giving the freedom to achieve more freedom'. However, Collins was now numbered among the many young leaders of promise killed in the civil war.

Cumann na nGaedhael Government

Apart from the draconian legislation it introduced to control unrest and political protest, much of it armed, the first Free State government under W. T. Cosgrave, leader of Cumann na nGaedhael, was not a very efficient one. After the assassination of O'Higgins in 1927, it became even weaker, and Fianna Fáil began to look a much more efficient organisation by comparison. The government seemed powerless to deal with the pressing social and economic matters, such as unemployment, poverty and emigration. It did back the country's first hydro-electric scheme – the Shannon scheme, near Limerick – and was also responsible for establishing the country's first sugar-beet factory in Carlow. But it did little or nothing to deal with the problem of housing, particularly in Dublin where the slums were a disgrace, and it actually cut the old age pension by a shilling a week in 1924.

However, in the field of public and even private morality it had strong views. These views coincided with those held by the Catholic hierarchy. Divorce was prohibited, a matter which was attacked with calculated savagery by W. B. Yeats, who was a member of the Senate. Also, the Irish Censorship Board, which was established in 1929, had the power to ban any work which was, in the opinion of the board's members, in its general tendency indecent and obscene. Any member of the public could set up a book for the distinction of being banned in Ireland by marking passages in three copies and passing them to the board. At one stage, the board was banning an average of three books a day and the list of books banned reads like a Who's Who of literature, old and new.

The chief sufferers were Irish writers, who seemed to be singled out for special hostility. All the outstanding Irish writers had works banned at some time and that meant that as well as being branded pornographers, they were also deprived of the benefit of sales in Ireland and cut off from potential readers. James Joyce, Seán O'Casey,

Seán O Faoláin, Frank O'Connor, Liam O'Flaherty, Edna O'Brien, Kate O'Brien and many more had works banned. The board even banned an English translation of a famous eighteenth-century poem in Irish *Cúirt an Mheán Oíche* (The Midnight Court) although it was available in the original.

There was also a rigorous censorship of films, but that was not at all as irksome as the censorship of books.

Needless to say, there was a strict ban on the importation or sale of contraceptives, and books and periodicals that dealt with what was known as 'artificial methods of birth control' were also banned.

Not until the liberal sixties were the censorship of publications laws relaxed and, although legislation still exists, the board now concentrates its attention on hard pornography.

Although this repressive legislation was introduced by the Cumann na nGaedhael government, their successors, under Eamon de Valera, did nothing at all to amend, abolish or ease it.

In the field of education, Fianna Fáil also followed the policy laid down by their predecessors. As in matters of public morality, the Catholic Church played a major part in the realm of primary, secondary and vocational education. This seemed logical, as the vast majority of secondary schools were owned and run by religious orders. But although the primary system was controlled by the state, at least in theory, all primary schools were managed by the clergy, who hired and fired the teachers.

Irish history was taught from the Irish nationalist viewpoint and Irish was made a compulsory subject in all first and second level schools and a failing subject in all state examinations. All governments followed this policy, established by the first Free State government, until a coalition government, headed by W. T. Cosgrave's son, Liam Cosgrave, changed the status of Irish in 1973. While remaining an essential subject it is no longer a failing subject in examinations.

Eamon de Valera

Fianna Fáil formed its first government in 1932 with the support of the Labour Party, on the understanding that the new government would introduce better social and economic policies than those favoured by Cumann na nGaedhael. Sinn Féin continued with its policy of abstention and its electoral support soon dwindled to nothing. De Valera immediately set about dismantling the aspects of the treaty he considered objectionable. First he abolished the oath of allegiance to the crown and the office of the governor general, the crown's representative who lived in the old Vice-Regal Lodge in the Phoenix Park, now the residence of the president of Ireland. He also refused to pay the land annuities – sums of money levied on farmers to reimburse the British government for compensation paid to landlords under the Land Acts – agreed in the treaty. This and other related actions led to a bitter economic war with Britain, which was the only market available to Irish agricultural produce. It was a severe blow to the cattle trade and the country's big farmers.

Cumann na nGaedhael took the farmers' side and it was at this time that a fascist-style organisation, called the Blueshirts because of the shirts they wore as a uniform, came into brief existence. The IRA, who thought they still had the power to manipulate de Valera, helped to break the Blueshirts, but when he felt the time was ripe de Valera moved against both organisations. The Blueshirts vanished, after sending an Irish brigade to fight for General Franco in the Spanish civil war. (Some socialists and republicans formed another Irish brigade to fight against him.) The IRA realised that de Valera in power was as likely to crush them as mercilesssly as he would any other organisation that got in the way of his political strategy; they went underground but remained active.

The Labour Party remained small and badly divided by splits between conservatives and mild socialists. It suffered from regular 'red scares', spread by its political opponents and latched on to by the Catholic Church. As a result of one anti-com-munist witch-hunt, there were two Labour parties in existence for a period. As there was no logical left-right division in Irish politics, the Labour Party remained weak and divided: other left-wing groups – until the emergence of the Workers Party – fre-quented the fringes of extra-parliamentary politics.

The 1937 Constitution

With an overall majority in the Dáil, de Valera introduced a new constitution in 1937, which is still in force today. Although it lays claim to the thirty-two counties as the territory of Ireland, it is effec tively a constitution for the twenty-six county state. However, northern loyalists see the claim as an implied threat to their state. The constitution de-clares that Ireland is a sovereign, independent, democratic state. It was accepted by a majority of voters in a referendum.

But, while it broke the last link with the British crown, the constitution stopped short of declaring a republic in the twenty-six counties. This step was taken by the country's first coalition government in 1949, when Fianna Fáil was put out of office for the first time. However, apart from some modifications – such as the removal of the clause giving a special position to the Catholic Church – each one requir-ing a referendum, the 1937 constitution remains basically unchanged.

An tUachtarán (the president) is head of state but has no executive function. The president may be elected by direct vote of the people, or agreed on by the political parties in Dáil Eireann, for a seven-year term of office, and is limited to two terms. Three of the state's first six presidents were elected by direct vote and three were agreed (including the first president, Dr Douglas Hyde). *An tOireachtas* (the national parliament) consists of the president, Dáil Eireann (the assembly or lower house, loosely translated as parliament) and Seanad Eireann (the senate or upper house). *An Taoiseach* (literally 'leader' in Irish) is elected by the Dáil, and is in effect the prime minister. All laws must be passed by both houses of the Oireachtas, must conform to the constitution and must be signed by the president before becoming effective. The president has the power to refer a bill to the Supreme Court if he or she has doubts about its constitutionality.

Dáil Eireann at present consists of 166 members called *Teachtaí Dála* (Dáil deputies or TDs) representing forty-one constituencies, of between five and three seats each, and elections take place at least every five years. Citizens who have reached the age of twenty-one may stand for election and all over eighteen have a right to vote. The system of voting is a fairly complex form of proportional representation, by single transferable vote, which makes most elections in Ireland as exciting as a protracted pursuit race. Its purpose is to ensure the fairest reflection of the widest range of political views.

If one takes a four-seat constituency (the number of candidates does not matter), for example, the voter places a 1 opposite the candidate of his or her first choice. He may then stop, or may place 2 opposite his next choice and so on until he has placed a number in front of every name. This means that if his first choice has no need of his vote, or if he or she has no chance of being elected and is eliminated, the vote is transferred to the voter's next choice and so on.

A quota is established by dividing the number of valid votes cast by the number of seats in the constituency plus one, and adding one to the total. For example, if 40,000 votes were cast in a four-seat constituency, the smallest number of votes necessary to elect a candidate would be: 40,000 divided by 5 (4 seats plus 1) +1, or 8001. If no candidate has reached the quota on the first count the one with the least number of votes is eliminated and his or her votes are distributed according to preference. This goes on until all seats have been filled.

Although Fianna Fáil introduced this system in the 1937 constitution, the party made two attempts to get rid of it in favour of the single-seat constituency with the straight voting system, but the electorate rejected the attempts in referanda. This system of PR does lead to tight situations. An overall majority of five in government is considered ample; anything bigger gives backbench members too much power. On the other hand the system can lead to situations where a single independent member may have the power to strike a hard bargain when he or she holds the balance of power. Its most marked effect in contemporary Irish politics is that it has led to the formation of some curious coalition governments that ousted Fianna Fáil. All of them brought together the Labour Party, supposedly socialist, and Fine Gael which is diametrically opposed to socialism. Fianna Fáil remained in power on its own from 1932 until 1948, when it was put out by the state's first coalition, and it has since remained the largest single party in the state, totally opposed to entering a coalition, but willing to accept support from other parties when it was needed, until that policy was modified by Charles J. Haughey when he took Fianna Fáil into coalition with the Progressive Democrats after the general election in June 1989.

In 1938 negotiations between Eamon de Valera and the British Prime Minister, Neville Chamberlain, resolved all remaining matters of contention between the two states, apart from the question of partition. Britain handed over three naval bases to the Irish government and relinquished all claims on defence facilities. The economic war was ended and a trade agreement between the two states was signed. All this meant that de Valera was able to call a snap general election and gain 52 percent of the votes cast. It left him in a particularly strong position when the Second World War broke out in September 1939. If neutrality in a world war is to be regarded as the ultimate exercise in national sovereignty, the seventeen-year-old state effectively asserted its role by declaring a policy of total neutrality as soon as hostilities commenced. Despite threats from the British and pressure from the Americans, de Valera, with the backing of all political parties in the Dáil and the vast majority of the Irish people, stuck to this policy. It meant imposing certain hardships, such as food rationing, shortage of fuel, compulsory tillage, and press and radio censorship. It also resulted in a big recruitment campaign to increase the strength of the armed forces and the establishment of an Irish merchant shipping fleet to carry essential supplies from abroad.

Neutrality had the effect of uniting the people in a cause to which the vast majority of them – apart from the IRA, and a small number of old unionists who were in favour of entering the war on the side of the Allies – could give allegiance. In that way it helped heal the wounds left by the civil war, as the sons of men who had fought on opposite sides joined the national army together. It also diverted attention from Fianna Fáil's obvious failure to implement what the party called 'the three great national aims': the re-unification of Ireland, the restoration of Irish as the everday language of the state and the ending of emigration.

The IRA decided to exploit Britain's difficulty by starting another military campaign, looking for support from Germany. The Fianna Fáil party, once described by Seán Lemass (who was to succeed Eamon de Valera as Taoiseach in 1959) as 'a slightly constitutional party' willing to come to an understanding with the IRA when it suited de Valera's purpose, now decided to crush the IRA mercilessly. Internment without trial was reintroduced, as well as the Military Tribunal that tried suspects in secret and a Treason Act that provided the death penalty for acts of treason. There were shootings, executions and deaths from hunger strikes and by the mid-1940s the IRA seemed to have been reduced to a small, ineffective group with little or no support from the public.

But when the war ended, the country's real problems emerged clearly once more. Emigration to the United States, ended temporarily by the war, began again on a large scale. Even greater numbers went to England, whose cities had to be rebuilt after Hitler's blitz. There was dissatisfaction too among the professional classes, particularly the teachers, because of poor pay. Sympathy for the IRA began to grow, mainly because of the circumstances surrounding the death on hunger strike of one of its leaders, Seán McCaughey.

Clann na Poblachta

All this led to the foundation of a new political party, Clann na Poblachta (Children of the Republic) under the leadership of Seán MacBride, once chief of staff of the IRA and later to become a noted international figure and winner of both the Nobel and Lenin Peace Prizes. In the general election of 1948 the new party, with policies remarkably similar to those of Fianna Fáil at its inception, won ten seats. Clann na Poblachta, in return for certain promises and two ministries, helped found the state's first coalition government with John A. Costello of Fine Gael as Taoiseach. Like his adversary Winston Churchill in Britain, de Valera, the father of his people in wartime, became leader of the opposition. Perhaps the simplest explanation for the defeat of Fianna Fáil in 1948 is that a majority of voters decided that after sixteen years of uninterrupted power, a change was needed – even for the sake of change.

The Republic Is Declared

The first basic change made by the new government was constitutional and a direct result of Clann na Poblachta's presence. The Republic of Ireland

Act came into force on Easter Monday 1949 with government politicians expressing hopes that this would 'take the gun out of Irish politics' for all time. The British response was to give the state of Northern Ireland a guarantee that 'in no event will Northern Ireland or any part thereof cease to be a part of His Majesty's dominions ... without the consent of the parliament of Northern Ireland'.

Far from removing the gun from Irish politics the declaration of a twenty-six-county republic had the effect of giving Sinn Féin and the IRA a brief new lease of life. A military campaign was launched in the last months of 1956 and led to the death in action of two young IRA volunteers, huge funerals and the participation in elections to the Dáil of Sinn Féin candidates for the first time since 1927.

The election was caused by Clann na Poblachta's withdrawal from the second coalition, because of the government's failure to solve the problem of partition. But the election was not fought on that issue but on the more pressing question of the country's grim economic position. The people gave Fianna Fáil yet another chance. Four Sinn Féin members were elected, refused to take their seats, and lost them again at the next election. Clann na Poblachta was almost wiped out and finally dissolved itself in 1965.

The IRA campaign petered out and died. Both governments, north and south, introduced internment and the military courts were revived in the south. However, the real reason for the campaign's failure was lack of real support from the nationalist community in the north; a fact that was admitted in the statement issued to announce the end of the armed offensive. The government and people of the southern state settled down to address the pressing economic problems. The Fianna Fáil Minister for Justice, Gerry Boland, once a member of the IRA, was able to assure the Dáil that the IRA was dead and that he was proud of the part he had played in killing it.

De Valera's Contribution

When Seán Lemass took over from de Valera, who went on to serve two terms as president, the emphasis was on economic matters: the development of the country's resources, the creation of employment and the task of attracting foreign capital for industrial investment. Although he was the dominant political figure of twentieth-century Ireland, Éamon de Valera, judged by what he set out to do, failed to achieve the three great national aims he so frequently quoted: ending partition, reviving the Irish language, ending emigration.

He saw the problem of partition simply as the occupation of six of the island's thirty-two counties by Britain. But having renounced violence as a means of solving the problem, he found himself co-operating with the Northern Ireland government in fighting the IRA while conducting an ineffective anti-partition campaign abroad, meant to bring pressure on the British government to agree to a united Ireland.

The revival of the Irish language, despite de Valera's undoubted personal commitment, had but a limited success and the use of the language outside the educational system did not increase perceptibly. From the foundation of the state it was a compulsory subject in first and second level schools and failing to pass it in state examinations meant failing the whole examination. It was also a necessary subject for entrance to the public service. That frequently meant that while a postman, for instance, had to have a knowledge of Irish, the minister in charge of his department was not subject to any linguistic regulation. Eamon de Valera never succeeded in infecting most of his cabinet colleagues with his own enthusiasm. But the most worrying aspect of the language problem was the decline of the Irish-speaking areas – *gaeltachtaí* – along the west coast, due to emigration and the commercial and social pressure of the English language. The state of the Irish language remains a contentious subject, but it is still the first official language of the state, as set out in the constitution.

Apart from setting up some native industries, and

protecting their products with tariffs, there was little economic activity during the years between 1932 and 1958. Agriculture followed the traditional pattern and there was no attempt made to develop a fishing industry, although the peat bogs were exploited for fuel and energy purposes and four hydro-electric power stations were built. It was not until the 1960s that a comprehensive policy for industry was prepared. Ironically, in view of what happened after the Anglo-Irish Treaty was signed in 1921, one of de Valera's great political achievements was that he proved the truth of what Michael Collins had claimed at the time: that the treaty contained the freedom to achieve even greater freedom. He created an independent republic in the twenty-six-county state in all but name. That he stopped short of calling it a republic was an effort to convince the British that a door had been left open, through an external relationship with the Commonwealth, which might lead to a solution of what he saw as an unnatural division of the island. It may have been a fond hope, but the declaration of the republic in 1949, if anything, made the northern state more secure and failed in its aim to take the gun out of Irish politics.

Seán Lemass

Seán Lemass was almost sixty when he took over from de Valera, and he was Taoiseach for seven years. The emphasis was on economic expansion. It was clear that something dramatic had to be done to revive the country's prospects. Emigration stood at about 50,000 a year, close to the annual birth rate. The programme for economic development was drafted by Dr T. K. Whitaker, secretary of the Department of Finance, and stated that risks would have to be taken if it was to succeed. Priority was given to export industries, and tax incentives were used to attract foreign capital. Various semi-state bodies – such as the Industrial Development Authority – were established to implement aspects of the programme and as the sixties progressed it was clear that the tide was turning.

Lemass, ever the laconic pragmatist, said that the rising tide of international growth in trading, and the prosperity it created, would lift all ships. Proof came in the census of 1966 which showed an increase in population of 52,000 and that the 20 to 25 age group had grown by 25 percent. Emigration had fallen to less than half of what it had been in the previous decade. People who had emigrated were beginning to return to a country that now seemed to have a bright future. A scheme to provide free second level education for all was introduced. The fiftieth anniversary of the 1916 rising passed without resurrecting the IRA, as some had feared, and the commemoration was largely confined to programmes on the new television service – Telefís Eireann – which had been established in 1960.

On the question of partition, Lemass made one practical gesture that seemed more significant at the time than it does with hindsight. He became the first Taoiseach to visit a northern premier. In 1965 he called on Captain Terence O'Neill at Stormont, and Captain O'Neill, who had the reputation of being a liberal, returned the visit in Dublin. It was seen to be in tune with the relaxed mood of the country at the time. When they met, Seán Lemass said, 'I shall get into terrible trouble for this!' Captain O'Neill replied, with what was prophetic accuracy, 'No, Mr Lemass, it is I who will get into trouble for this.'

For reasons which have never been fully explained, Seán Lemass announced his retirement from politics quite suddenly in 1966, with no obvious successor in sight. This led to a power struggle inside Fianna Fáil, the aftermath of which lasted for years after Jack Lynch became party leader and Taoiseach.

Jack Lynch

Lynch, a pleasant-mannered Corkman who had served in a number of important ministries, was known nationally as a brilliant hurler. He gave the impression of being a reluctant candidate among a pack of ambitious and ruthless office-seekers. Charles J. Haughey, son-in-law of Lemass, was favoured by a section of the party, but the retiring Taoiseach gave no indication that he favoured him or any other prospective candidate. In his first election, in 1969, Lynch proved his worth as a vote-getter by winning an overall majority for Fianna Fáil against almost all predictions. His rivals inside the party seemed to have little choice but to back him fully and he seemed set fair for a successful and trouble-free term of office.

His main preoccupation was Ireland's entry into the European Community (EC), which was being negotiated, and the maintenance of economic growth. The prospects looked good. For the first time in the history of the state the numbers returning to the country from abroad, particularly from Britain, exceeded those emigrating. A young generation was being educated for employment at home. For most of them emigration was no longer a necessity, or even an option to be considered.

The central flaw in the development of industry in Ireland, however, was that it relied to an unrealistic extent on enticing foreign companies to Ireland by offering them favourable short-term tax incentives. Many of them left again as soon as the tax holiday ended. But before he had time to settle into office as Taoiseach in his own right, Lynch was caught in the one situation for which he was least prepared. The north exploded and neither Lynch, nor the party of which he was leader, had even the semblance of a policy to deal with the crisis.

Northern Troubles

Some historians maintain that the partition of Ireland is not so much a cause of strife as a symptom of something that existed long before the northern state was established, and that the British presence is not the cause but the result of a deep division between communities. It can be said with truth that the colonisation of east Ulster in the seventeenth century succeeded all too well. Not alone did the descendants of the settlers not assimilate, but they retained almost intact the siege mentality of settlers in a hostile land. Two aspects of the conflict puzzle outside observers and bewilder many Irish people as well. The first is the role of religion: is the conflict religious or political in essence? The second concerns the attitude of the loyalists to the British government: why are they so frequently at odds with the will of the Westminster parliament if they are both British and loyal, as they claim to be?

The conflict is not a religious one and neither side has any wish to convert the other, but it does contain a strong religious element, ever since the plantations of the early seventeenth century and the war of 1641. Most loyalists are of the Protestant persuasion and almost all nationalists Catholic. And while most of the Catholic bigotry tends to be political in origin, a lot of the more virulent Protestant bigotry is rooted in anti-Catholicism. The annual commemoration of King William's victory over the Catholic King James, at the Battle of the Boyne in 1690, is more a triumphalist ritual than a joyful celebration.

The state was established in 1922 as the lesser of two evils (the other being a united Ireland) under the threat of civil war from the loyalists. Instead of the nine counties of Ulster, six were chosen to form the state, as they seemed to ensure a self-perpetuating Protestant majority. Even as the state was established the warning signs were there and the British prime minister, David Lloyd George, in 1922, drew attention to the fact that in the previous two years four hundred Catholics had been murdered and twelve hundred wounded, without a single person being brought to justice. Nevertheless the British government gave control of the organs of administration, including a huge armed police force, to one section of the community and without restraint from Westminster, as Northern Ireland had its own parliament at Stormont. The Stormont government manipulated constituencies by gerrymander to ensure that the minority got even less than fair representation in local and general elections. The loyalists justified their distrust of Roman Catholics, who had no choice but to share the state with them, on the grounds that they were basically disloyal, supported the IRA and wanted the new state merged with the rest of the island under a Dublin government. After the failure of the IRA campaign in the late fifties, coupled with the arrival of Terence O'Neill as prime minister, it seemed that an attempt would be made to deal with Catholic grievances. Catholics were beginning to show signs that they would no longer be willing to put up with second-class citizenship.

Captain O'Neill tried to convince the Unionist party that if Catholics were treated in the same way as Protestants they would begin to behave like Protestants, particulary in matters of family planning. The traditionally large Catholic families were widely regarded as a threat to Protestant numerical supremacy in the future. In response to the demands of the militant and well-organised Civil Rights movement (inspired by the marches and songs of the black Civil Rights movement in the USA) Captain O'Neill introduced some mild reforms giving the Catholics a better deal in the allocation of local authority housing and public appointments. He was immediately attacked by the extreme wing of the Unionist party, which turned out to be a majority and not a wing, and by the Rev. Ian Paisley, who had formed the more extreme Democratic Unionist Party. O'Neill was accused of being a traitor and preparing the way for an united Ireland. He was eventually forced out of office.

On the nationalist side a new type of politician came to the forefront. Bernadette Devlin, a young student from County Tyrone, emerged suddenly as a parliamentary candidate and was elected to Westminster. She created a sensation by bringing the conflict into parliament and by having scant regard for parliamentary conventions. On one occasion she rushed across the floor of the House and boxed Reginald Maudling's ears. When asked by a reporter afterwards if she was not ashamed of herself, she said she was only sorry that she had not choked him. Another, more enduring figure on the nationalist side, was John Hume from Derry, who became even better known internationally than Bernadette Devlin.

It was in Derry that the police first responded to a peaceful Civil Rights march with a baton charge. Derry was the most glaring example of gerrymandering in local elections in Northern Ireland. Because of careful manipulation of the electoral map, two-thirds of the population which was Catholic (and nationalist) and one-third Protestant (and unionist) elected a corporation two-thirds unionist and one-third nationalist.

Television pictures of the events in Derry were shown all over the world. Even after a decade of peace and quiet the Northern Ireland government was unable to respond to moderate requests until the situation had degenerated into street violence.

Catholic streets in Belfast were attacked and burned and, as the police made no effort to protect them, Citizens Defence Committees were set up. As the IRA had all but vanished, representatives of these committees were sent to Dublin to ask for guns to defend nationalist areas. In Derry the police ran amok through the Catholic Bogside, breaking into houses and beating people indiscriminately. This led to the arrival of the first British troops who were welcomed as protectors by the nationalists.

The plight of the beleaguered Catholics led to a major crisis in the Dublin government and the dismissal of two of the most prominent ministers in Jack Lynch's cabinet, Charles J. Haughey and Neil Blaney, on suspicion of importing arms (to be used to defend Catholic areas in the north) illegally. They were acquitted after a sensational trial. The problems of Northern Ireland began to cast a deeper than usual shadow over political life in the republic.

The European Community

In 1971-72, however, the burning issue in all parts of the republic was membership of the Common Market, as the European Community was then known. As far as the two major parties were concerned there was no alternative to membership. The largest occupational group in favour of joining was the farming community. The benefits to them were obvious. Not so obvious were the benefits to industry, but the attraction of money from the social and regional funds was also strong. Those in favour of entry also argued that Britain and Ireland as members together would be able to discuss the northern problem regularly, in a wider context. But the most conclusive argument in favour of membership was that on its own – and deprived of access to the British market if they joined without Ireland – the Irish economy would be destroyed.

Although the media gave the anti-Marketeers' case a lot of space and air-time, it only had the backing of small political groupings and individuals who were forced to fall back on the nationalist argument that Ireland should be master of its own destiny and seek its own markets and allies. Even the Labour Party was not united in what was supposed to be official opposition. But where the opposition to membership failed was in putting a clear alternative to what was generally perceived to be the overwhelming argument in favour of membership before the electorate. The result of the referendum was sufficiently clear to effectively put an end to a major argument about membership. In May 1972, 83 percent of those who voted in the referendum were in favour of joining and membership became effective in January 1973.

Initially the farmers, whose expectations of EC largesse were highest, were more than pleased with higher prices for cattle, sheep and dairy produce.

Their increased prosperity seemed to complement the prosperity of other sections of the community. The allocation of money for regional development also made a difference, although it was noted in time that not all available grants were utilised because of inadequate advance planning. The fledgling fishing industry found it difficult to accept some of the regulations imposed in the interests of conservation and the fact that some traditional fishing grounds had now to be shared with better-equipped competitors.

Some traditional industries, such as the Ford motor works in Cork, were forced to close and, more worrying still, some of the newly-arrived industries – attracted by generous grants and other incentives – began to depart. With the advent of the oil crisis the tide that lifted all boats began to ebb, leaving them high and dry. Some economists warned that state spending in the creation of non-productive public service jobs was too high and that the money borrowed to create them would one day become a national liability. But in the 1977 general election, Fianna Fáil, under Jack Lynch, gained the biggest overall majority in the history of the state by taking rates off houses and road tax off cars.

Economic Crisis

As is frequently the case in Ireland the crisis came out of a relatively clear sky, so far as the government was concerned. Suddenly, everyone was complaining that the economic miracle was at an end and that nobody had warned them. The prosperous farmers soon realised that they were producing that which the European Community had in abundance: dairy products and beef. Unemployment among industrial workers increased as a result of more and more closures, and inflation soared as state spending raced ahead of income. Jack Lynch, the most popular leader since de Valera, was the first casualty. After losing two by-elections in his native Cork he resigned as Taoiseach and another power struggle inside Fianna Fáil began. It was much more bitter than the one that had accompanied his own election and its aftermath more prolonged.

Charles J. Haughey, whose prospects of leading the party seemed by many to have been destroyed by the arms trial, as well as a lengthy period on the back benches, won the party leadership and became Taoiseach. One of his first acts was to address the people on television and radio to warn them that the country was living beyond its means and that the foreign debt would have to be cleared. As the people braced themselves for a savage budget, all that happened was a series of attempts to oust Haughey from the leadership. This campaign ended when his main opponents inside the parliamentary party broke away to found a new party, the Progressive Democrats. If de Valera was the

Houdini of twentieth-century Irish politics, Charles J. Haughey must have been its Lazarus.

This was a period of many general elections, with minority Fianna Fáil governments alternating with coalitions between Fine Gael and Labour, with the new leader of Fine Gael, Dr Garret FitzGerald, as Taoiseach. On economic policy there was no disagreement in principle between Fianna Fáil and Fine Gael: the government's financial affairs had to be rectified and drastic reductions in state expenditure in all areas – particularly in health, social welfare and recruitment to the public service – were recommended. There is no doubt that a Fine Gael government with an overall majority would have implemented that policy, but its Labour partner could not agree to severe cuts in social welfare and medical expenditure. The Fianna Fáil answer to Fine Gael was that there was another way out of our problem, without being too specific about what it was.

When getting into power, however, Fianna Fáil made even deeper cuts in public expenditure and made the lowering of inflation and the elimination of the national debt the cornerstone of their economic policy. To a great extent, financial policy became the greatest single issue to polarise the political parties in the republic as the end of the century and the implementation of the Single European Act approached. The vast majority of elected representatives in the Dáil belong to parties that favour financial rectitude and the reduction of public service expenditure. The minority, an uneasy collection of left-wingers of varying hues, favours mildly socialist policies, while a minority within that minority favours more extreme ones.

Northern Conflict Grows

The conflict in the north grew increasingly violent through the 1970s as the new prime minister, Brian Faulkner, tried to hold on to power. He persuaded the British government that the introduction of internment without trial would crush the newly-resurrected IRA. That resulted in a major outbreak of violence all over the north and particularly in Belfast. A new grouping of anti-unionist politicians came together, encouraged by the Dublin government, to form the Social Democratic and Labour Party (SDLP) which was anxious that nationalists should have a democratic outlet for their aspirations in constitutional politics.

Shortly after internment was introduced the SDLP withdrew from Stormont because of the fatal shooting of two unarmed men in Derry and the British government's refusal to hold an inquiry. It was now clear that the situation was getting out of hand. On 20 January 1972 thirteen unarmed civilians were killed in Derry when British paratroopers opened fire on a crowd protesting against internment. It was a turning-point.

The British prime minister, Edward Heath, abolished Stormont and decided to rule the state directly until such time as a different kind of assembly could be set up. Under much pressure it was decided to include the Dublin government in the discussions, and a tripartite conference was held in December 1973 between representatives of the British and Irish governments and both sections of the community in the north. This led to the establishment of a power-sharing executive, representative of one strand of unionism (a minority, led by Faulkner himself) and a larger strand of nationalist opinion. It took office in January 1974 with Brian Faulkner as leader.

It worked well for a few months but was weakened by a change of government in Britain and unfavourable election results in the north and was eventually brought down in May 1974 by politically-motivated industrial unrest by loyalists, led by Ian Paisley and the extreme unionists. The British government, under Harold Wilson – who once drew up a ten-point plan for Irish unity – refused to use the army to provide essential services such as electricity. The executive fell and that brought to an end the only attempt to involve the two communities in running the northern state.

In the following years there was little political

movement in the north and violence continued at varying degrees of intensity and horror. Many politicians, in Britain and in both Irish states, seemed to regard violence – and particularly IRA violence – as the problem rather than a symptom of a much older problem. When violence declined the British government seemed to regard it as an indication that the IRA was close to defeat, but they failed to avail of periods of relative peace to further political activity.

When violence erupted the authorities reacted with increased security measures. One result of this was that the IRA seemed to occupy the centre of the stage, capable of escalating its campaign of violence, at home and abroad, at will. Because of a change of policy, Sinn Féin (the IRA's political wing) entered into democratic politics, mainly in local government, polling about 10 percent of the total vote. This, in turn, served to contradict the theory that the IRA had no support in the Catholic communities. The Protestant para-militaries, such as the Ulster Defence Association (UDA), and its off-shoots, such as the Ulster Freedom Fighters (UFF) and Ulster Volunteer Force (UVF), did not seem to be regarded by the authorities as posing the same threat to security as the IRA. The UDA was not a proscribed organisation.

Hunger Strike

While events in the north had an effect on aspects of political life in the republic from time to time (the burning of the British Embassy in Dublin in 1972 after the Bloody Sunday shooting in Derry; and the loyalist bombing of Dublin and Monaghan in 1974, killing thirty civilians), and while the troubles imposed a strain on the legal and penal systems, they remained surprisingly remote and became an election issue on one occasion only since 1968. This was during the mass hunger strike in the Maze Prison, near Belfast, in 1981-82.

The hunger strike grew out of the protest against the abolition by the British government of the special category – the political prisoner. The prisoners affected by this refused to wear prison clothes or obey prison rules. They wore blankets and covered the walls of their cells with their own excrement. The protest became known as the 'dirty protest', but in the vocabulary of the prisoners and their supporters it was known as being 'on the blanket'.

The hunger strike produced one major martyr for the IRA among the ten men who died. This was Bobby Sands, who was elected as an MP to the House of Commons while on hunger strike, and whose funeral attracted a huge crowd. He refused to take his seat in parliament, following Sinn Féin's policy of not recognising a 'foreign' assembly, but his death made a deep impression abroad (streets were named in his honour in Teheran and in Paris) and at home it proved to be a major influence in recruiting volunteers for the IRA

H-Block candidates (H-Block describes the shape of the buildings in the Maze Prison) stood in the election to Dáil Eireann in June 1982. Some were elected and others succeeded in polling enough votes to deprive the Fianna Fáil party of a overall majority in that election. In the election that followed, in November of that same year, Fianna Fáil was defeated and replaced by a coalition under Dr Garret FitzGerald as Taoiseach.

The strike and the attendant street protests also politicised Sinn Féin, and the party won seats on local councils all over Northern Ireland. They accepted these seats and in fact the party controlled some town and county councils, polling about 10 percent of the electorate. The hunger strike ended when the parents of some of the strikers intervened, as it was then clear that Mrs Thatcher was not going to agree to their demands. It was at this time that the IRA is believed to have decided that it would assassinate the British prime minister. They came close to doing so during the Conservative Party conference in Brighton in November 1984.

But, although it became obvious the longer the northern conflict went on that border security was placing a heavy burden on state expenditure and that some solution would have to be arrived at, it was as if the majority of people in the south wished the problem out of sight and out of mind.

Financial Rectitude

After the general election of 1987, Charles J. Haughey's government became a minority government – depending on the support of a few independents. Haughey decided to impose severe cut-backs in state expenditure in all areas and, as inflation fell and income began to exceed expenditure, his popularity and that of his government soared to such heights that the opposition had to be careful not to defeat him on an important issue and give him an excuse to call a snap election. But in one important area these policies had no immediate effect. Financial rectitude did not create employment, at least in the short term, and emigration rose to levels comparable to that of the 1950s.

The only difference was that the new generation of emigrants were on the whole better educated, equipped with a much wider range of practical skills and, as a result of membership of the EC, had the choice of a greater variety of countries in which to seek work. Still, the USA was the country most favoured by those who sought longterm security. The problem was that the Irish quota for permanent emigrants to the USA had become very small, with the result that the country contained thousands of young Irish emigrants who were working illegally. One of the main problems facing any Irish government, as the end of the twentieth century approached, was to procure more and more work visas for those contemplating emigration as well as for those already working illegally in the USA.

Southern Policies on Northern Ireland

Even if the majority of the electorate in the republic seemed reluctant to face up to the problems of the apparently endemic violence and lack of political movement in the north, their political leaders continued to seek a solution. Garret FitzGerald, who had written extensively about the northern question, seemed to favour an internal settlement inside the existing state, coupled with some sort of All-Ireland dimension.

Charles Haughey, on the other hand, referred to the northern state as a 'failed political entity', and this was taken as total commitment to a united Ireland in some undefined form. Both leaders had meetings with the British prime minister, Margaret Thatcher – some that seemed to hold promise, others that led to acrimony. All Irish politicians of the nationalist persuasion, north and south, were united in condemnation of her method of dealing with any crisis in Anglo-Irish affairs by making strident public pronouncements which were then echoed and exaggerated by the most undesirable sections of the British popular press.

The Anglo-Irish Agreement

The Anglo-Irish Agreement signed in Hillsborough, near Belfast, in 1985 came as a result of the perseverance of the SDLP leader, John Hume, in applying pressure on politicians in Britain and the USA and of the refusal of Garret FitzGerald to take Margaret Thatcher's persistent resistance to any political change in the North as a final answer.

Under the agreement, which was rejected out-of-hand by the loyalist politicians with their usual 'No', the Dublin government was able to make representations to the British government on matters affecting the northern minority. Regular meetings were held between ministers from both governments and a permanent secretariat was set up near Belfast to operate the working of the agreement. Despite the fact that it reiterated the British government's guarantee to loyalists that they would not be forced into a united Ireland, they saw it as a step in that direction.

Albert Reynolds succeeded Charles Haughey as Taoiseach in 1992. Negotiations between Reynolds and John Major, the British prime minister, resulted in the Downing Street Declaration in December 1993. It stated that the British had no selfish, strategic or economic interest in Northern Ireland. The

British government agreed that it was for the people of the island of Ireland alone, by agreement between the two parts, to exercise their right of self-determination, on the basis of consent freely given.

John Hume's initiative in opening talks with Gerry Adams, leader of Sinn Féin, was widely criticised, but the IRA ceasefire of August 1994 followed and was generally believed to have been influenced by those talks. Two months later the loyalist paramilitaries also declared a ceasefire.

Throughout 1995, difficulties regarding decommissioning of IRA arms hindered the start of the all-party talks. In November 1995 John Bruton, the new taoiseach, and John Major agreed to establish an international body, under US Senator George Mitchell, to conduct an independent assessment of the decommissioning issue.

Resulting from multi-party negotiations, including the British and Irish governments, political parties representing the two communities in Northern Ireland and parties linked to the paramilitary groups from both sides, the Good Friday Agreement, also known as the Belfast Agreement, emerged on 10 April 1998.

This agreement doubly assures the Unionist community that Northern Ireland 'remains part of the United Kingdom and shall not cease to be so without the consent of a majority of the people of

Northern Ireland.' The Irish government undertook the amendment of Articles 2 and 3 of the Constitution, Article 3 to recognise 'that a united Ireland shall be brought about only by peaceful means with the consent of a majority of the people, democratically expressed in both jurisdictions in the island ...'

The agreement was followed by referenda held in both parts of the island. The electorate of the Republic and of Northern Ireland (both communities) voted in its favour, the vote in the Republic exceeding 94 percent.

Efforts continued to set up the executive government of ten ministers, plus the First and Deputy First Minister, in accordance with the agreement. Decommissioning of paramilitary arms, particularly those of the IRA, continued to be a problem despite the closest attention of Tony Blair, the British prime minister, Mo Mowlam, then Secretary of State for Northern Ireland, and US Senator George Mitchell. Under the agreement, decommissioning was to be handled by an independent commission, chaired by Canadian General John de Chastelain.

Though a final solution remained elusive, the Good Friday Agreement greatly advanced the possibility of its early realisation. The efforts of those concerned in the protracted negotiations were not in vain. Greater understanding grew between Northern Ireland's two communities. Once unable

to meet in the same room, Unionists and Nationalists began at last to talk.

David Trimble and Seamus Mallon were
appointed First and Deputy First Ministers respec-
tively. However, it took another year and a half
before it became possible to implement the Agreement. Unionists insisted on the decommissioning
of IRA arms before they would agree to enter the
new executive government with Sinn Féin.

Finally, in December 1999, agreement was
reached. The Northern Ireland Executive
Government was established. It consisted of representatives of the Ulster Unionist Party (UUP), the
Social Democratic and Labour Party (SDLP), Sinn
Féin and the Democratic Unionist Party (DUP).
David Trimble undertook that, if the arms decommissioning process had not begun by February
2000, he and the Unionist Party ministers would
leave the executive government. The IRA
appointed a representative to work with the
Independent International Commission on
Decommissioning.

The other new institutions envisaged in the
Good Friday Agreement could now be established.
The North-South Ministerial Council provides for
meetings between ministers from Northern Ireland
and from the Republic, and for intergovernmental
work on a range of issues. The British-Irish
Council provides for regular meetings between

representatives of the two governments and the devolved institutions in Northern Ireland, Scotland and Wales, together with representatives from Jersey, Guernsey and the Isle of Man.

The British-Irish Intergovernmental Conference was launched by the taoiseach, Bertie Ahern TD, and the British prime minister, Tony Blair MP, and provides for regular meetings between representatives of the two governments.

In December 1999 Peter Mandelson, the British Secretary of State for Northern Ireland, published a report: *Security – Return to Normality*. The report sets out the British government's 'overall strategy for achieving normal security and policing in Northern Ireland'. It was the fervent hope of the people of both parts of Ireland that the unique moment in time which marked the end of the twentieth century – and the end of the millennium – would also mark an end to strife, and the beginning of a new era of harmony and peace, in the island of Ireland. But the institutions were suspended by the British government in February 2000, and direct rule from London reimposed, in a move designed to stave off David Trimble's resignation and the potential unravelling of the Good Friday Agreement.

Ireland Today

In the last decades of the twentieth century Ireland has experienced radical changes, socially, morally and financially. Taken together, these changes have greatly influenced the outlook and the living standards of the Irish people. Once a rural society whose priority was land ownership, a flight from that land new prevails. Young people are no longer prepared to undertake the struggle associated with life on the land. This attitude has added to the problem of increasing urbanisation.

The recent historic upturn in the Irish economy has created overcrowded towns and cities, their urban sprawl spreading destructively over the surrounding countryside. In Dublin, for instance, an out-dated infrastructure is no longer capable of meeting modern demands, and the gridlocked traffic is now believed to be costing the economy over one billion pounds per annum. Successive governments failed to predict the ever-increasing love affair of the Irish people for their cars.

Until the mid-1980s Ireland was beset by the size of its national debt, the high level of its taxation and the continual rise in unemployment. The only escape for young people was emigration, and it occurred on a massive scale. The current economic boom has transformed that age-old pattern into a new phenomenon, that of immigration. With a newly bouyant economy, Irish employers are now in need of workers to fill their vacancies. A recent survey by the Economic and Social Research Institute reported that over 50,000 job vacancies existed in all sectors of employment, but were greatest in the high-tech manufacturing sectors.

Not alone are emigrant Irish coming home, but British and Continental workers are also arriving in large numbers. The resultant rising population, particularly in Dublin, has created an urgent need for living accommodation, a situation exploited by landlords and property vendors. This in turn has let to unhealthy over-borrowing by young people in their extreme efforts to set up homes. As a way out, commuting has become the norm for many, sometimes from as far away as Carlow, Mullingar and Drogheda. This has resulted in demands for better transport services.

The new prosperity brought by the so-called Celtic Tiger has also introduced a new prodigality, one which verges on the reckless. The current philosophy seems to be 'eat, drink and be merry', without regard to the possibility of a future bursting of the economic bubble. Two cars, two foreign holidays and wine in plenty are part of the expectations of the new middle-rich. This rampant consumerism has attracted British and foreign commercial interests prepared to compete in the booming Irish economy.

The new attitude to modest wealth may well be influenced by the revelations of several tribunals of enquiry which have shocked the nation. Illegal financial dealings over years on the part of trusted figures and institutions have been exposed. These include bankers, business executives and corrupt politicians. While in the 1980s the people were being told to tighten their belts, and PAYE workers had no alternative but to pay up, some in the higher echelons of society were practising tax avoidance and evasion on a grand scale. The tribunals of enquiry continue in the lengthy process of investigating these scandals.

Time was when the Roman Catholic Church would have thundered its disapproval of such corruption, but as it is still smarting under the lash of criticism of its own scandals, the voice of rectitude is now more often heard from the Church of Ireland.

Like the reunification of Ireland, the revival of the Irish language, another of de Valera's great aims, has failed. Though it is the first official language of the State, as set out in the Constitution, it never became the spoken language of the people. This is partly because of the element of compulsion associated with its teaching in schools.

However, there is a new and growing interest in the language. Due to lobbying by parents, some schools are being funded to teach through the medium of Irish. Television is helping to popularise the spoken word, and its attraction has also been strengthened by the astonishing revival of traditional Irish music which began in the 1960s. Traditional Irish music is now popular throughout the world.

As elsewhere, drugs and crime flourish amongst the deprived. The less deprived fail to acknowledge that alcohol, an over-used drug, continues to be responsible for over one-third of our road deaths. Having outlived most of their inhibitions, the Irish now keep their divorce courts busy, and contraceptives have become part of teenage life. Abortion continues to be a highly emotive subject.

Boom-time Ireland never had it so good as at the close of the twentieth century. The hope is that prudence will prevail in mapping the road to a happy and prosperous future for all of Ireland's people.